PEOPLE AND PLACES IN BRISTOL

Introduced by
E. V. Thompson

BOSSINEY BOOKS

First published in 1986
by Bossiney Books,
St Teath, Bodmin, Cornwall.
Typeset, printed and bound
in Great Britain by
A. Wheaton & Co., Exeter.

ISBN 0 948158 13 1

Plate Acknowledgements

Front Cover: David Mansfield
Back Cover: Julia Davey
Julia Davey: pages 5, 10-17, 20, 63, 80, 85-108
Rosemary Clinch: pages 18, 45, 46, 49-53, 58, 60
Gloucestershire County Cricket Club: pages 9, 25, 67-74
Mark Foot: pages 31 lower, 36, 37
Michael Clinch: pages 42, 48
Diddie Williams: page 55
George Gallop: page 76
David Clarke: page 7
Mildred Ford: page 56

Contents

Introduction

by E. V. Thompson

E. V. THOMPSON is one of the most famous novelists living and working in the Westcountry. He has achieved huge national and international success with novels like Chase the Wind *and* Ben Retallick. *He served in the Royal Navy, and his latest novel is* Polrudden. *His earlier Bossiney titles are* 100 Years on Bodmin Moor, Discovering Bodmin Moor *and* Discovering Cornwall's South Coast.

It was with very real pleasure that I accepted an invitation from Michael Williams, publisher of Bossiney Books, to write an introduction to People and Places in Bristol. Although I now live much deeper in the heart of the Westcountry, Bristol – 'The Gateway To The West' – has always held a special place in my affections, for a number of reasons.

My introduction to Bristol came when I was a very small boy. My father brought me here from London, just he and I, to stay for a couple of days and a night. When we travelled together it was always a great occasion for me and Bristol came up to all my expectations. We had a look at the ships moored in the docks just off the city centre – there were many more of them in those days – then explored the ancient gateway of Saint Bartholomew's hospital and the steepness of Christmas Steps and went to a film in the evening – for the benefit of cinema buffs, the film was *Typhoon*, starring Dorothy Lamour. By the time we were heading back to London along the A4 road, Bristol had become a magic memory in a small boy's mind.

Right: *'In its heyday ... one of the country's greatest sea ports ... host to many famous people ...'*

Many years later I was to return to Bristol as a policeman, my beat covering the same city centre, Christmas Steps and part of the remembered dockland. I also partrolled the residential areas of Kingsdown and St Paul's. This was to prove a fascinating and ·illuminating period of my life.

It was here, too, that I had my first short story published and took the first, uncertain footsteps along a path that would eventually lead to authorship and a way of life that leaves me envious of no man.

I thought up the idea for my short story as I walked the area bounded by Bristol's ancient city wall in Bell Lane on one side, and the wider thoroughfare of Baldwin Street on the other. The story was typed at 2 a.m., when other policemen were enjoying a meal and a brief game of snooker before returning to the streets to face the cold of a winter night. The life of a policeman provides a wonderful grounding for a storywriter. His experiences are many, varied – and frequently unexpected.

In *People and Places in Bristol*, Rosemary Clinch writes of some of the city's present-day 'personalities'. Bristol has always had a great many men and women who might best be referred to as 'unusual characters'.

One such man I have never forgotten was an ageing 'gentleman of the road'. Known popularly as 'the flower man', he always wore a selection of wild flowers in his button-hole. Sometimes it would be so large it would trail down to his waist. Under his arm he carried a battered biscuit tin. When we first met I was a young, inexperienced policeman. In the early hours of the morning in Stokes Croft, not far from the junction with Jamaica Street, I asked him what he had in the biscuit tin. I regarded his reply, 'Photographs of my mother-in-law', as being unnecessarily provocative. I suggested he might like to show them to me, believing I was 'calling his bluff'. Leading me to the circle of light cast by one of the older-type street lamps, he opened the tin and I spent a somewhat embarrassed half-an-hour making polite remarks about the matronly lady portrayed from middle to old-age in a series of cracked, sepia-coloured photographs.

'The flower man' and I met frequently during subsequent years

Right: *Author E. V. Thompson: 'Bristol has always held a special place in my affections ...'*

and, after I had left Bristol, I saw his own photograph peering at me from inside the pages of *The Countryman* magazine. It seemed that my wandering friend, with his tin of treasured photographs, was as well-known in the country as he was on the streets of Bristol.

There were many such characters to be found in the city in those days. Percy and Selina, who had a stormy yet strangely devoted relationship in the twilight world of the penniless and homeless; one-legged Joe, who was wont to wield his crutches as though they were battle-axes and who had a disconcerting habit of entering Bristol's restaurants and ordering a gigantic meal, complete with cigar. The meal over, Joe would lean back, replete and momentarily at peace with the world, and admit he had no money with which to settle his account.

The lifestyle of Joe, Percy and Selina was shared by many in those days. One evening I stood in the shadows of an upstairs window in a derelict house in St Paul's and watched a whole army of vagrants going to ground in the ruins of houses destined for slum-clearance. It made a great impression on me. By the time I left the uniform branch for plain-clothes duties I knew each of the vagrants by name and had listened to the stories of a great many. Sadly, I was able to improve the lot of only a very few.

Most of the derelict houses have gone from Bristol now, and the army of city vagrants is no more than a memory. It is better so.

Of course, there have been very many more 'solid' citizens of Bristol. Men and women whose names are familiar to its residents, and those who visit this fascinating and historic city. Men like John Cabot, the Genoese explorer, who sailed from Bristol in 1497 on an historic voyage that led to the re-discovery of Newfoundland and Nova Scotia, long forgotten after its probable discovery in 1000 AD, by Leif Ericson, son of the Norseman, Eric the Red. This was about the time when Bristol's history as a seaport was just beginning. Cabot returned to England to receive as his reward from King Henry VII the miserly sum of ten pounds.

Admiral Penn, father of the founder of Pennsylvania in the United States, had a home here. So too did Coleridge – and the poet

Right: *W. G. Grace in 1895. 'I scored 1000 runs with this bat' was the inscription on this photograph.*

laureate, Robert Southey was born here. Both these poets planned a utopian colony on the Susquehanna River in Pennsylvania, but their ideas of an earthly paradise came to nothing.

Explore the narrow lanes behind St Mary Redcliffe Church, Queen Elizabeth's 'Fairest, goodliest and most famous parish church in England' (quite as true today as it was then). Here, on the wall of a modest house in the shadow of the great church a plaque tells us that Samuel Plimsoll was born here. Known as the sailors' friend, he was the originator of the Plimsoll line which put an end to the dangerous overloading of merchant vessels.

In its heyday Bristol was one of the country's greatest sea ports. As such it was host to many of the most famous people in the land.

Bristol has been a major seaport since earliest times.
Left: *Divers continue the seagoing tradition today.*

But what of the true sons and daughters of the city? Bristolians who left something tangible for those would come after them?

High on this list must surely be John Harvey, the founder of 'Harveys of Bristol', now a world-famous name wherever good wines are enjoyed. Their superb ports and sherries are still housed in Denmark Street, in cellars that were ancient when John Harvey first made use of them.

Many years ago when I was policing Denmark Street in the early hours of the morning I heard unusual noises coming from the cellars of the newly-opened Harveys restaurant. Climbing the railings, I dropped down into the basement and set off to investigate the sound. It turned out to be nothing more serious than a young university student, employed by the company to spend the night washing-up. His salary was augmented by as much food as he could eat, and a generous supply of wine. I called in to check on his well-being on a number of occasions during the dreary, quiet, early-hours of the months that followed, and I date my partiality for good wine from those brief encounters with the products of the Harvey cellars.

The cellars beneath Denmark Street are quite extensive and may be visited by prior arrangement with Harveys. Perhaps one day someone may draw up a map and delve deeply into the history of this area of Bristol's hidden past.

It was another, earlier wine merchant who willed the money for a bridge across the Avon gorge. William Vick was the wine merchant, but the name that has become synonymous with the Clifton suspension bridge is that genius of engineering design, Isambard Kingdom Brunel. It is ironic that Brunel never lived to see the completion of this, one of his earliest engineering projects. The building of the bridge was, not surprisingly, dogged by problems and this remarkable engineering feat was not completed until 34 years after Brunel submitted his original design.

The Clifton suspension bridge is not the only heritage this brilliant engineer has left to Bristol. It was he who brought the Great Western Railway to the city. His genius may also be seen in Temple Meads station, scene of countless farewells and joyful

Left: *Clifton suspension bridge. Brunel never lived to see its completion.*

homecomings during the eventful 150-year-old history of the GWR.

Yet another proud example of Isambard Kingdom Brunel's inventive genius is the SS *Great Britain*. Now open to visitors in the very dock where she was constructed and launched in 1843 by Prince Albert, the vessel was the world's first propeller-driven iron ship. In length 322 feet, and of 3,270 tons, the SS *Great Britain* was a marvel of her times. The vessel's subsequent history, and the story of its recovery from the Falkland Islands are stories too well-known to be repeated here. Nevertheless, the tenacity shown in returning this unique vessel to the place of her conception and birth would surely have been appreciated by the man who built this great ship.

A less welcome visitor to Bristol, way back in 1327, was Edward II. Perhaps it would be more accurate to refer to him as the 'late' King Edward II. Murdered in Berkeley Castle, seat of the Earls of Berkeley, his body was refused burial at the Abbey Church of St

Left: *'Yet another proud example of Brunel's genius is the SS* Great Britain.*'* Below: *Sion Hill viewed from the suspension bridge.*

Augustine's, established almost two centuries before by an earlier lord of Berkeley Castle. Such partisanship came close to bringing financial ruin upon the Abbey. The king's body was buried in nearby Gloucester Abbey instead, his shrine becoming a place of pilgrimage and bringing both wealth and fame to Gloucester. However, despite this, St Augustine's Abbey Church has survived to become Bristol's cathedral.

The city is well-endowed with churches, but the lofty magnificence of St Mary Redcliffe still tends to steal much of the glory from Bristol's less-spectacular cathedral.

A church that is a particular favourite with me is Temple Church.

'Bristol is well endowed with churches ...' Left: *St Mary Redcliffe.* Right: *Temple Church.*

Hit by German bombs during World War II, the church is now little more than a shell but, in common with a certain building in Pisa, its tower leans at a discernible angle.

The bushes surrounding this ancient church once provided a sanctuary for those vagrants who felt in need of something.... perhaps a little 'up-market' from St Paul's. One I recall owned a vintage perambulator in which he kept all his worldly possessions. During the day he might be seen pushing it around the city centre. At night this resourceful 'Gentleman of the Road' would take off his boot and, without removing his sock, would tie a string to his naked big toe. The other end of the string was attached to the handle of his ancient baby carriage and until dawn he was a living burglar alarm.

When excavations were being carried out inside Temple Church I would often pay visits on night duty to view the skeletons of long-dead Bristol personages. An annual service is still held in the church and it is of interest to know its bells may still be heard in the city. Taken to the cathedral, they are once more in regular use.

17

'Rosemary Clinch writes of some of the city's present-day "personalities".' Ivor Morris, coachman.

Another church which I found of great interest in those not-too-far-off days was yet another bomb-damaged place of worship. This was the church of St Mary-le-Port, which stood close to Bridge Street. Excavations were carried out here too and the discoveries were of Bristol's very earliest days as a busy port. Sections of a Saxon road were exposed, together with graves of the same period. These too were duly examined in the light of my police torch and I never failed to leave there with a feeling of awe at having viewed the mortal remains of men and women who had walked the cobbled streets of Bristol more than a thousand years before.

Bristol has been a major sea port since those earliest times. It has witnessed drama, changing fortunes, and not a little human hope and misery. For many years it was the main port from which prospective settlers set sail for America. Some left the shores of their native country filled with hope for a wonderful new future. A new beginning. Others sought nothing more than escape from the miseries of their present existence. Yet undying memories of Bristol were carried across the Atlantic Ocean by many thousands of these emigrants and the result is that no fewer than twenty communities in the brave new world bear the name of 'Bristol'. No doubt a great many of their descendants are among the thousands of visitors who come to the city each year.

But Bristol saw other travellers who set off for America without any of the hope that sustained the emigrants. These were slaves, human merchandise taken from their villages in Africa and bartered in the ports of that vast, dark continent. Packed tightly into holds, each allocated no more than the space they might have had in a coffin, commerce and not comfort were the only considerations of the slave-merchants. It is known that most ships plied direct from Africa to America and the Caribbean with their cargoes but, when I was a wanderer around the quays and jetties of old Bristol I was shown an opening in the cliff-face, above one of the Redcliffe wharves. Here, slaves were supposed to have been placed whenever a slave-ship called at the port.

Certainly, Bristol merchants were involved in the slave trade during the eighteenth and nineteenth centuries, and many families grew rich on the proceeds. Some actually kept slaves at their great houses and a few were released from bondage here. It is doubtful whether many slave owners emulated the Earl and Countess of Suffolk. The couple lavished great care on a certain Scipio

*The Llandoger Trow still retains the 'feel' and the
traditions of an inn with three centuries of seafaring
clientele.*

Africanus, whose elaborate headstone may still be seen in Henbury
churchyard.

Jillian Powell contributes a chapter entitled 'Churches and Inns' (a delightful coupling) to this book. She has chosen subjects that have contributed a great deal to the city's colourful history. We have already touched briefly upon my own interest in some of the many churches to be found in the city. I find the history of inns equally interesting.

In common with sea ports the world over, Bristol's inns were justifiably famous wherever sea-going men gathered. Two of the oldest inns remaining in the central area of the city must surely be The Hatchet, in Frogmore Street, and the seventeenth-century Llandoger Trow, sited within a comfortable anchor's throw from the Welsh Back quayside.

The area around The Hatchet – now known as '1606' – has changed beyond all recognition in post-war years. It is a far cry from the days when the celebrated bare-fist pugilist Tom Cribb trained here with his cronies.

Times may have changed for The Hatchet, but the Llandoger Trow still retains the looks, the 'feel' and the traditions that go with an inn which has been associated with a seafaring clientele for more than three centuries. It is believed to be the inn on which 'The Spyglass', Long John Silver's tavern in *Treasure Island* was modelled. Here too, Alexander Selkirk related his experiences as a castaway on the uninhabited island of Juan Fernandez to author Daniel Defoe. The story became the famous novel, *Robinson Crusoe*, beloved by schoolchildren, and now frequently seen on British stages during the pantomime season. I too have made use of the inn – using its real name – in my own novel, *The Restless Sea*.

Pass by the Llandoger Trow on a dark, stormy night, when the wind is being channelled along the Avon gorge from the Severn estuary and you can almost hear the clanking of pewter pots, and the singing of sea-shanties. Through these doors have passed seafaring men whose Westcountry accents have been heard in every sea port throughout the world.

Not many paces from the Llandoger Trow, and its junior by no more than a century, is the Theatre Royal, the oldest theatre in Great Britain. Opened in 1766, the theatre houses the Bristol Old Vic company and can claim that some of the most famous names in the world of the theatre have trodden its ancient boards.

I have always been fascinated by the many facets of the theatre and have enjoyed reading David Foot's contribution to *People and*

Places in Bristol, devoted to the theatres of Bristol. I was pleased that he includes a mention of the brilliant, yet tragic actor, Edmund Kean. This unhappy little man – he was five feet four inches tall, would have known Bristol well. Kean married at nearby Stroud, when he was nineteen, the money for his wedding licence being borrowed from the theatre box office. Kept short of money by his mode of life, Kean was forced to walk from one place to another to take up many of his acting engagements. His unfortunate young wife frequently accompanied him, even when she was heavily pregnant. Yet, in spite of his many shortcomings and human weaknesses, Kean was a formidable actor. As David Foot writes, 'Bristol.... was fortunate to have seen him.... at his most brilliant best.' Perhaps Kean's ghost is one of those reputed to haunt this most respected of theatres.

There are other theatres and halls in Bristol and, when I lived in the city, I would often watch artists and actors at rehearsals. I once watched Cliff Richards rehearsing, during his first British tour. I forecasted that he was unlikely to make the grade in his chosen profession! Occasionally it is a pleasure to be proven wrong.

I have also been fortunate enough to meet a number of the personalities who have found fame through appearances on the stages of theatres throughout the world. Sir Harry Secombe; Ken Dodd; the late Matt Monroe; George Cole and Frankie Vaughan among them. As a uniform policeman I once suffered the embarrassment of watching Lonnie Donegan from the wings of the Hippodrome while a thief raided his dressing-room and stole his wallet! I have watched performers in various states of nervousness, or apparent unconcern as they waited to walk those terrifying few paces to the centre of the stage to face a new audience. I greatly respect their dedication to a highly competitive profession. I entertain no doubts why those who achieve recognition reach the top in the world of entertainment. It is sheer hard work, guts and determination.

This is equally true of those who dedicate their lives to sport – and Bristol has never been short of such men and women. Being hardly more than a drop-kick away from Wales, it is hardly

John Gielgud as Prospero and Michael Feast as Ariel in
The Tempest *at the Hippodrome.*

surprising that Bristol should have a fine tradition of Rugby Union, producing many fine players.

Jack Russell is contributing a chapter to *People and Places in Bristol* and, as a professional sportsman, he knows what can be achieved when talent is married to determination. His sport is, of course, cricket. Gloucestershire, the team for whom he plays, has fielded some of the greatest cricketers of all time.

First and foremost of Gloucestershire cricketing personalities must be that grand old man of the sport, William Gilbert – 'W.G.' – Grace. The standard of sport has risen dramatically in recent years. Consequently, many of our young cricketers must be considered to be the best we have ever known, but it is doubtful whether any cricketer before, or since, has achieved the stature of 'W.G.'

Born at Downend in 1848, 'W.G.' was trained for the medical profession and was an able doctor, but it is as a cricketer he is remembered – and small wonder! In 1871 he scored 2,739 runs, his average being 78 runs per innings. He is best known for his batting ability, but his record of more than 2,800 wickets taken during his career proves he was no mean bowler. On one occasion, when playing against Oxford University, he took all ten wickets in one innings, at a cost of just under five runs per wicket.

Many other sporting activities take place in Bristol – even I confess to having taken the field with a hockey stick in my hand on behalf of Pegasus – and many Bristol sportsmen and women through the ages have found fame. In addition to Tom Cribb, the early prizefighting ring produced men of the calibre of Henry Pearce, Bristol's 'Game Chicken', Jem Belcher and John Gully who left the ring to become a Member of Parliament and make a fortune from horse-racing. More recently, Robin Cousins set new standards in the world of ice-skating and Jo Durie is making her mark on the world tennis circuit. But I must let Jack Russell tell the story of Bristol's sporting personalities in his own way. He shares the pages of this book with Jillian Powell, David Foot and Rosemary Clinch. Each is writing about one of the very many varied aspects of this great city. A city that has given much to the world in the past, and is certain to contribute much more in the future.

I would once lean my elbows on a wall in Park Row during the night hours and think of the greatness that has been woven into the fabric of Bristol's long history. Of the men and women who had given their lives to the city. Looking out over the shadowy spires,

*W. G. Grace is introduced to the Prince of Wales after a
cricket match at Windsor Park.*

silent factories and warehouses, inns and theatres – and the houses
where live the inheritors of Bristol, it gave me a great feeling of
pride. For a few, slumbering hours I, and perhaps two dozen others,
were responsible for protecting this priceless heritage.

A heritage of sports personalities; actors; actresses and theatres;
inns and churches. A heritage I shared for a while with the famous
and with the equally important, but less well-known personalities.
All have helped to make Bristol the city we know today. All have
contributed something to our own lives. May this book, in its own
modest way, achieve something of the same.

Theatres of Bristol

by David Foot

DAVID FOOT writes regularly on cricket, soccer and Rugby for various newspapers, including The Guardian *and* The Sunday Express. *He has worked in radio and television and is the author of several books. His* Harold Gimblett, Tormented Genius of Cricket *is rated one of the finest books of its kind. 'There has never been a cricket book quite like this,' wrote John Arlott. 'David Foot has written it with compassion, something not too far from passion, and sympathy. It is a remarkable achievement ...' In 1984, David Foot wrote the Introduction to* Strange Somerset Stories *and contributed a chapter entitled 'Midnight Poachers at East Coker'.*

Whenever I think of the Bristol stage, my quirky mind turns to Charles Macklin, that extravagant and tetchy Irish actor. He was famous for his Macbeth, his Shylock and his Iago – to Garrick's Othello – and toured regularly in the Westcountry, where he won rapturous applause. He demonstrated a jealous nature and a roving eye.

Macklin was, I recall, reluctant to quit. He was almost ninety when he last played Shylock. It wasn't that an Irishman couldn't assume the role of a Jew any longer. Old age and a fading memory clouded his ill-advised performance. He was still on stage, stumbling through his words, when the manager walked on and called it a day.

I don't think Macklin ever 'dried' in Bristol during his talented and colourful career in the eighteenth century. But he did once

Left: *David Foot, theatre reviewer for thirty years.*

cause a minor scandal during a visit of his company to the old, claustrophobic theatre in Jacob's Well. He chose a programme which allowed him to be absent for a large part of the evening. It was an arrangement, according to contemporary rumour, very much to the liking of the manager's nubile daughter in an adjacent bed-chamber.

The small playhouse in Jacob's Well, alongside Brandon Hill, was Bristol's first permanent theatre. It was built in 1729 because John Hippisley had the vision to realise that wealthy people coming to Hotwells to take the (suspect) waters might also like to see some of the country's great tragic actors – and sample melodrama and other thespian entertainments – at the same time.

This cramped theatre had minimal comfort or hygiene. But it was a gesture to the Arts in the city. Bristol was getting a bad name: there were too many fat merchants, too many philistines. Jacob's Well at least recognised other values in life. It also embraced conviviality. The audiences could be boisterous. There were reports of how ale would be passed through a hole in the wall from a nearby tavern. All was fair. The theatre was outside the city boundary.

Hippisley himself must have been something of a character. He was born near Wookey Hole and had hints of a Somerset accent that he'd obscure as he strode ambitiously into some juicy acting parts in his own right. He must have been talented. In London he had played Peachum in the original production of *The Beggar's Opera.* He was strong on comedy – and business acumen. For a time he ran a coffee-house in case he ran out of engagements as an actor. He relished the entrepreneurial role and ensured there were attractive bookings of his London company at Jacob's Well.

But the place simply wasn't big or grand enough. Chatterton, the precocious poet, wrote that it was no more than a hut. It was, in fact, a good deal more than that. There was need, however, for a new, larger theatre – to ensnare an emerging theatregoing public in Bristol. The puritans weren't happy: they still saw the public stage as a meeting place for lewd behaviour and coarse levity. But the foundation stone of the Theatre Royal, in King Street, was laid in May 1766. Today the building is the oldest working theatre in the country.

That long history has, of course, been strewn with financial trauma, political in-fighting, petty jealousies and conflicting interests. There have been bad managements – and bad actors. Not

An interior view of the Theatre Royal, Bristol.

all audiences have gone in search of cultural enlightenment. At least once in the 1830s, the police had to be urgently summoned because of noisy and drunken behaviour in the auditorium.

In one of her booklets on the theatre, Kathleen Barker told us what happened during Macready's farewell performance of *Lear* in 1850: 'The dramatic corps and the audience were surprised to observe a black terrier dog protruding his glossy head from out of a private box, in which sat three military officers who were endeavouring to excite him to give an audible manifestation of applause...' The great Macready noted the canine competition. It hardly pleased him. What was the military coming to? But then, what did soldiers know about Shakespeare?

There was always, in the early days, an interchange between Bath and Bristol. It worked out well. A company could, with careful timing, manage a performance in both cities on the same day. That was if the cast stayed judiciously away from liquid stimulants.

This wasn't easy in the case of the dissolute and compelling Edmund Kean, who made his first appearance at Bristol in 1815. Here was a tragic actor on the grandest of scales, contemptuous of the sheer notion of underplaying anything. His acting skills were prodigious. So were his sexual appetite and drinking capacity. He was dead by 46 – and Bristol, like Bath, was fortunate to have seen him, often sober and at his most brilliant best.

Sarah Siddons also became proficient at the shuttle service between the two Theatre Royals. She made many friends, outside the theatre, in Bristol. There were stories of her rather haughty backstage manner. She loved the ambience of King Street and generously bequeathed her ghost to her successors. I used to know a wardrobe mistress with the Bristol Old Vic who swore she had seen it.

Business rivalry between Bristol and Bath was inevitable. Bristol clearly had the edge when it came to measuring the respective opening nights. Bristol was launched with *Conscious Lover,* directed by William Powell, who had transferred from Jacob's Well. Powell was a capable actor and a friend of Garrick.

The friendship was valuable. Garrick tried out his doggerel for a specially-written prologue. He sat in the audience, led the applause and said some heady things about the beauty of the new building and the prospects for it. Rather surprisingly, his initial enthusiasm wasn't followed-up, as hoped for, by a professional visit. Most of the other leading actors came, at some time.

So that was Bristol's launch. Bath's, in 1805, was altogether less memorable. The management went for a big one, *Richard III.* It also had an extraordinary aberration. An unknown amateur was cast as Richard. His name was never revealed. He was described naively as someone making his first appearance on the stage. And so it looked. He forgot his lines, took countless prompts and became utterly demoralised long before the end. The audience became restive.

But it strikes me, the whole theatre has been punctuated by

Above: *Clive Wood
appearing as Henry V in
the Bristol Old Vic
production of 1982.*
Right: *The Theatre
Royal today.*

31

aberrations. They are often almost engaging in their own embarrassing way. The critics, quite apart from the mystified audiences, are left shaking their heads. As a theatre reviewer for thirty years, I have often tried to divorce my journalistic instincts from the job – not easy after a lifetime in the trade. It is best to come fresh and open-minded to the play, not privy to the rehearsal anguish and frantic re-working.

Only once have I been threatened with physical violence. That was when I, in company with most of the other local reviewers, was less than charitable about a farce given its première at the Bristol Hippodrome in the late fifties. The piece was quite appalling and pulled out every cliché known to man. The sexual innuendo was distasteful and the only worthwhile diversion was, I recall, the appearance of an ash-blonde of prodigious proportions who did her honest best to take our minds – at least our eyes – off the so-called dramatic happenings on stage.

The playwright was on the phone, in fighting mood, almost as soon as the ink was dry on the first editions next morning. On another occasion, the normally amiable Frankie Vaughan left me in a state of confused silence as he phoned to tell me just what he thought of the previous day's notice of his bill-topping performance in variety at the Hippodrome. At last I managed to blurt out that he was talking to the wrong man – I'd delegated the show to another reporter on my evening paper – now, incidentally, a high-powered television executive.

There were apparently perks for the more resourceful critics, even the outspoken ones. I'm thinking of the stage-struck Bristol architect Edward William Godwin, friend of Whistler and of more than one comely actress. He married twice but his great love was still Ellen Terry. She first met him when he invited her to one of his famous teas or soirées. The delicate friendship grew to the verge of scandal.

In the mid nineteenth century, the busy architect and socialite somehow also found the time to be a regular writer on the theatre for the *Western Daily Press*. His notices were vitriolic. He was a stickler for accuracy in design according to the period. Some of his criticism about what he saw at the Theatre Royal was unfair. It was said he never had a bad word to say for a Terry. Not all critics end up as lovers to the great actresses of the day, of course.

The 'Royal' was taken over by the Arts Council in 1942 and

became what was in effect a Bristol division of the Old Vic four years later. It has grown to be one of the great regional companies. In 1966, the lovely building was two hundred years old; in the early seventies it was briefly closed and reopened as an extended theatre centre, featuring the Georgian Coopers' Hall and incorporating a new downstair studio with a flexible auditorium.

Garrick may have chosen not to play King Street but almost everyone else did – from Irving to Rogers and Neville, Porter and Sinden. The cobbles reek of theatrical romance. I only wish I'd seen some of the tatty revues and Randolph Sutton's long-running Christmas shows, as well as the heavy plays that came later. But at least I was, figuratively, in the wings to witness bizarre moments to cherish.

In the pub across the road, during a rehearsal period when creativity was not progressing as it might have, a pint of beer was poured onto the head of a well-known composer... by the musical's co-author. Peter O'Toole, still untamed and mightily talented, would make this same pub with five minutes to spare before closing time. He'd then down a succession of draught stouts as only an Irishman could.

O'Toole was 24 when he played Hamlet. He lost two stone in the run-up to opening night. To my surprise he phoned me the day before and asked me to come out for a drink. He was in a tense state and had been given a few hours off. 'Let's talk about professional football,' he said, 'anything but Hamlet'. His father had briefly been a goalkeeper with Sunderland.

I'll pluck just two other memories of O'Toole. He had gone with the Bristol Old Vic to London, when the musical *Oh, My Papa!* transferred. There was a large Westcountry contingent in the audience at the Garrick and they applauded and stamped their feet joyfully through the numbers. Up in the gallery, theatre politics were at work. An organised group of first-nighters seemed to be doing their best to wreck the show. I went backstage afterwards and found some of the cast in tears; they couldn't understand what was happening.

O'Toole tapped me on the shoulder. His language was expressive. It said, in effect: 'I'm going to find those noisy buggers from the gallery even if it takes me all night. Stick around and you'll get a story.' It wasn't easy as I had my wife, eight months pregnant, loyally by my side. We stayed with the hawk-eyed actor and a few

33

other heavies till just before midnight, by which time I had to catch the last train back to Bristol. Peter O'Toole's last words to me were: 'You'll be sorry you missed the action.'

In my newspaper office next morning I read an agency report that the flamboyant actor had been fined ten shillings at Clerkenwell for being drunk and disorderly in Holborn at 2.10 a.m. A charge against his sister Patricia, of obstructing the police, was dismissed. It was reported that O'Toole and four of his mates had been drinking stoneware beakers of home-made mead. I don't know from where they got it: they hadn't moved onto honeyed products when I left them.

There was also... the cricket match. It was the Press against the Actors. Bristol Old Vic has, in fact, always taken its cricket seriously. I used to walk along the narrow alley-way, that previously led to the stagedoor, in the lunch-hour and could be sure that Leonard Rossiter – left arm slow – would be organising an improvised match with a tennis ball. But back to O'Toole, fearsome right-arm fast, of dubious length and line.

The match was due to start at 2.30 and the actors arrived marginally late by way of the Portcullis and other Clifton watering holes. Pretty young actresses were there as camp followers. We batted – and O'Toole retired to deep third man, refusing to move at the end of each over. But then a strange thing happened. An ageing Bristol critic, resplendent in newly creased flannels, walked to the wicket with bat in hand at first wicket down.

O'Toole emerged from self-induced slumber and indicated he was ready to bowl. He came in off a run of 35 paces, all arms and legs and Lear-like incantations. It was a superb delivery and all three stumps went over. The critic walked glumly back to the pavilion. The bowler walked back to deep third man. 'All I ever wanted to do,' he informed his doting followers.

I suppose I was – and am – stage struck, just like Godwin had been more than a century earlier. At times I found actors insufferable company en masse, when they limited their conversation to the theatre and became increasingly camp. Individually they were often great fun. They never had any money and were not a good bet when it came to buying a round. They

Right: Peter O'Toole who did two periods with the Bristol Old Vic.

*Colston Hall with the once-thriving and much-loved
Little Theatre up the stairs at the end.*

never wanted to go to bed. Norman Rossington slept in an old barge, moored at Welsh Back, just across the road from the Bristol Old Vic.

Their keenness to accept your hospitality could be disconcerting. The first interview I was sent on by my theatre-conscious news editor was with the late Rachel Roberts. She was a Baptist minister's daughter and I suspected she might be an abstainer. That was a serious error of financial judgment on my part. She showed a distinct partiality to Martinis. As I worked for a struggling paper, my expenses account was painfully modest. I learned to conduct future theatrical assignments, in those callow journalistic days of mine, out of pub hours.

Some of my happiest times came in covering the plays at the Little Theatre. The Rapier Players were formed in 1935 to keep the Little going; they reluctantly terminated their lease from the Bristol Corporation in the summer of 1963. We all shed tears together but losses since 1957 had made the parting inevitable. Only Liverpool and Birmingham had had regular repertory of this kind longer than Bristol.

The Hippodrome nestling among shops in St Augustine's Parade.

The Little had a seating capacity of only 450 and that ruled out large profits with the most successful shows. But the artistic standard was high under the direction of founder Ronald Russell and his wife, Peggy Ann Wood. They selected their plays astutely. Their approach was intimate and friendly. The public's affection for the company was real but the Rapiers looked in vain for help and subsidy.

Ronald Russell and Peggy Ann Wood said their sad goodbyes and returned to freelancing with deserved success. Both appeared, ironically, with the Bristol Old Vic; Peggy Ann was seen often on television. Meanwhile the BOV used the Little Theatre as an additional outlet for a period. It was never a wholly practicable arrangement and was quietly dropped. A brave, talented breakaway group, calling themselves the Little Theatre Company, took over residency. They won critical acclaim but they, too, ran out of money.

Out of this climate of uncertainty we come to the Hippodrome, now under new and confident management, Apollo Leisure. Oswald Stoll's splendid touring theatre was opened for the first time in 1912. It was the best and, many said, the most handsome place of entertainment outside London. Eugene Stratton topped the first bill. There were water spectaculars. W. C. Fields came and so did Sarah Bernhardt, direct from the London Coliseum.

How I'd have loved to see Little Titch, G. H. Elliott and Vesta Tilley there. But I did catch up with Gracie Fields, Sandy Powell, George Formby and Max Miller. Vic Oliver introduced me to his latest girl friend. Terry-Thomas got in a state because the hyphen had been left off his name on the big posters outside. The marvellous Jimmy James directed me away from himself and said: 'That's the lad to talk to. He's only joined me this week and he's going to be a star.' Name of Roy Castle.

It was a big, flamboyant theatre with lots of backstage space. As such it was ideal for pre-London try-outs of new musicals. Noel Coward came to see *Sail Away* and the Master granted me an interview in Row K during rehearsal. *Annie Get Your Gun* opened here and so did *The Music Man,* with Van Johnson. There were G and S, variety, straight plays, rock'n'roll and ice shows. Once, as the market turned fickle, there were films.

Often one detected tension. The uneasy relationship between Lucan and McShane – Old Mother Riley and her daughter Kitty – was well known. Twice I eavesdropped on storming rows among double acts renowned for their warm affinity. A talented, underrated Jewish comedian, Freddie Bamberger was so grateful for the write-up I gave his shoestring show that he rung and invited me to a private end-of-week party he was throwing for his chorus girls. Robert Luff sent me an LP of the Black and White Minstrels, who had opened for the very first time in Bristol, at the Hippodrome. Those examples were the nearest I ever got to being corrupted.

Bristol is a city rich in theatrical tradition. Apart from the beautiful Theatre Royal and the lavish Hippodrome, we have professional fringe – Avon Touring – and consistently good work at the University's Glynne Wickham Theatre. I'm no more highbrow than the day I reviewed, both eager and apprehensive, my first Shakespeare in King Street. I like it all: if the standard is high. Frankie Howerd once told me his one ambition was to be accepted

Right: *Danny la Rue topping the bill at the Bristol Hippodrome.*

as a Shakespearean actor. Many classical performers admit they are tremendously envious of an old-style vaudeville trouper who can do a funny walk and crack one-liners for twenty minutes all on his own.

I'd have loved to wallow in much of the mighty and unmitigated ham that masqueraded as acting in the grand manner through the closing years of the eighteenth century and then the nineteenth. There was the famous story of a peacock-proud actor who was so pleased with one of his soliloquys during a Westcountry visit that he stopped, took a bow and repeated it two more times. The rest of the cast just put their hands on their hips and waited with well-practised forbearance.

It's a great regret of mine that I came along too late to join in the boisterous bonhomie at the People's Palace in Baldwin Street or one of the other supposedly down-market music halls where post-Victorian performers broke free from a fettered morality and unleashed a tirade of innuendo and risqué rhyme. It was part of the radical change-around in this country.

For centuries, Bristol's disregard of the Arts was an embarrassment. It may have been the 'second city' in the land – but not when it came to artistic sensitivity. Then even the corpulent merchants of Clifton became smitten by conscience and sheepishly took themselves off to the emerging theatre.

Bristol for me would be only half a place without the theatre. Moira Shearer put away her ballet shoes to act here. Harry H. Corbett left his rag-and-bone cart to play Macbeth here. Charles Macklin... but that's where we came in.

Characters of Bristol

by Rosemary Clinch

ROSEMARY CLINCH made her debut for Bossiney in 1984 contributing a chapter entitled 'Strange Sightings and Mystical Paths' in Strange Somerset Stories. *She followed it as co-author of* Unknown Somerset *and in 1985 wrote Bossiney's first Bristol title* Unknown Bristol *which fired David Foot in his Introduction to comment: 'I get the firm impression that Rosemary Clinch relishes looking round the corners and under the pavement stones just like I do. She's happy to leave others to write the official and more obvious words about Bristol.' More recently she has written* Supernatural In Somerset. *Rosemary is married and lives near Bristol.*

I am fascinated by people, their lives and occupations – what makes them 'tick'. Maybe my grandfather sowed those early seeds, for he had one of those knees I would willingly occupy to listen to his colourful tales and he taught me 'to be seen and not heard'. 'After all,' he would say, 'you never know what you might learn!' But it took a dedicated though perhaps overworked Bristol magazine editor to 'fire' a latent enthusiasm some years later, as I pondered over a feature problem. 'Don't just sit there,' he shouted. 'Get out and rout 'em out!'

Today, I still delight in the tales on fame, fortune and even felony which make up Bristol's historic past but I find a special thrill in the untold stories of people still living who are generally lesser known. Behind a face or figure which catches my eye, chance meeting or intended introduction, might be a personal account worth the telling. As I 'rout 'em out', the past and present, reality and romance are proffered with enthusiasm, punctuated by moments of wit, or even 'tongue-in-cheek'. Every story I am told creates a picture, one piece in the enormous jigsaw of life in and around the

city. These are the stories of three people who contribute a special richness to Bristol, whether behind the scenes of notability or as an average resident of 'chez-nous'.

The ordinary Bristolian of the past possessed a vigorous pride and helped to forge a reputation which made Bristol throughout history independent of other cities. I have a strong impression that the people of Bristol today will continue this tradition.

IVOR MORRIS

In the harness room at Ashton Court stables I was surrounded by the scent of polished leather and brass and an atmosphere going back more than 500 years.

Through a doorway from the stalls came the restless stamping of horses' hooves on cobbles, reminding me of how proud chargers once pawed the ground, clad in chain mail, carrying fearsome spikes on their brows. But the harness hanging in neat rows on the wall was not of that age nor were the glass coach lamps which sat gleaming on a shelf in a large cupboard.

I had approached this magnificent house through beautiful parkland, an estate of more than 800 acres. Here, the people of Bristol can wander at will, follow nature trails and picnic. They can sit contemplatively in the gardens among roses and colourful herbaceous borders while in a quiet corner under an ancient tree lies a collection of small graves, edged with stones and carrying the names of the Smyth family's pets. It is the illustrious Smyth family who will be remembered most among the owners of Ashton Court.

I had come to see Ivor Morris, the Lord Mayor's Coachman. For 25 years he has carried out his duties as Head Coachman to a succession of Lord Mayors, being responsible for the care of coaches and horses and driving the Mayor in fitting style to civic ceremonies and functions. The stables are part of such an historic building full of memories and yet not permanently occupied, and I wondered what it was like for Ivor and his wife living in the flat above. Although the house is available for conferences and public

Left: *Author, Rosemary Clinch.*

functions, its massive, long and slender construction allows the stables at the rear to be a very private place.

'I have not seen any ghosts,' Ivor said with a smile. 'It is very nice living here. It doesn't bother me at all but the atmosphere can be heavy at night. Some time ago, late one evening, we had a surprise visit. We wondered who on earth it was and, when I looked outside, I could see a taxi. From the dark an American voice said, "Excuse me, is there a room in there with a black marble mantelpiece?" Well, you can imagine I thought the fellow was off his head! I said there was and the voice said, "That was my office!" It turned out he had been stationed here in the war and supplies including jeeps arrived by boat at Avonmouth and were brought to Ashton Court for storage. He was thrilled to bits to see his old office again. Since then I have had visitors from all over the world looking round but I will never forget that night.'

Ivor was born in 1926, a Bedminster boy, living in Cabot Street. He grew up with horses which in the 1930s were still a common sight on the streets of Bristol. It was not surprising he was eventually to share his life with them.

'My grandfather and my father worked with Corporation horses used for transport. In those days they had Sunday morning transport, so I would often help. I remember twenty or thirty different types of trader still used horses in those days.'

During the war Ivor served with the Royal Horse Artillery. He travelled through France, Belgium and Holland while sharing a special kind of companionship, caring and providing the necessary human attention a horse needs in unsettled circumstances. After the war, he left the service and spent time as a lorry driver but his love of horses soon found him working at a local riding school until eventually he arrived at the Lord Mayor's door of the Mansion House.

'Ronald Steer was Head Coachman before me,' Ivor said. 'He came from London and returned to work at Buckingham Palace in 1960 and that was when I was lucky to be appointed. At that time the stables were at Clifton near the Mansion House. When the Corporation acquired Ashton Court, the house and stables were in such bad repair, we only kept the horses here at first and left the

Right: *Ashton Court.*

coaches and harness at Clifton. If we had a function to attend, I would have to ride one horse while leading the other up to Clifton before preparing the horses and carriage, then afterwards, I had to ride and lead the horses back to the Court. It was certainly a lot easier when the house and stables were refurbished and we moved everything down here.'

As Lord Mayor's Coachman, Ivor's life is a very busy one. Harness needs regular cleaning, keeping leather supple and brass gleaming. There is also a large amount of it. 'It's like the Forth Bridge,' he said. 'By the time you get to the end, you have to start again!' Pointing to some sets hanging at the end of the row, he said with obvious pleasure, 'They were only used once, for the Bristol to London Bicentenary Mail Coach Run driven by John Parker. I thought it would be nice to have the harness back in Bristol so eventually we were able to purchase them through the Guild of Guardians, whose aim is helping to provide traditional items for Mayoral use.'

Always a splendid sight, is the pageantry of coach and horses in procession conveying the Lord Mayor through the city and I wondered if Ivor had a particular favourite out of the many occasions when his service is required.

'Oh yes,' he said, 'Rush Sunday at St Mary Redcliffe Church. There is so much colour and the feeling of expectation, the coming of summer, sea and sun. But there are other events too. When some of the Queen's horses came here to be stabled on her visit to Bristol in 1977, we really worked hard to look good for that occasion. What a wonderful time it was. Then again, we took horses and carriage to Hanover for a Grand Parade, an important event really, being able to represent the City of Bristol abroad. In 1982 we attended the Lord Mayor's Show in London and Remembrance Sunday.'

Replacing another well-cleaned bridle on its peg, Ivor reflected again.

'You know, all the Lord Mayors never lose touch with me. They are always appreciative of the work I do looking after the horses. If a horse goes lame or sick, they are as concerned as I am, but now we have Dutch Geldalanders the horses are not so bad.'

Ivor has two daughters, Jackie and Julie, and a son Phillip. Like

Left: *Ivor Morris with Samuel.*

The Author talking to Ivor Morris.

her father, Jackie has a love of horses and is a keen competition driver but living in Australia means contact by tapes and videos to keep up with family news and events. A visit 'down under' was quickly accepted by Ivor when asked to attend as a judge at the Royal Melbourne Show. 'It will also give me a chance to promote Bristol again,' he smiled.

Under the expert and kindly guidance of Ivor, helpers at the stables can learn the best of horse and stable management. Cheerfully going about their duties is Maxine Challis a young lady on a Youth Training Scheme Course and a young man, keen to join the Army, known affectionately to Ivor as 'Fusilier' Fuller, 'Saturday mornings only'! 'Darren Fuller has been with me for six years now,' he said. 'Then there is Mrs Anne Ames. She has been a great support to our present efforts with her expertise, having been involved with the Dodington Carriage Museum.' Then Ivor told me about sixteen-year-old Sarah Heddington from Hartcliffe. He has just reason to be *very* proud of her winning a place at the prestigious Windsor Driving and Coaching School.

'She had only been here at the stables for ten months on a Youth Training Scheme. She was horse-mad *and* a wonderful worker. It all began when I was at the 1985 Royal Windsor Show and happened to be talking about Dutch horses and the need for good grooms. I told them I had the finest little girl in England and not long afterwards I was taking her up to Windsor for an interview. What a thrill it was for me and the City Council when she got the job. We are all so proud of her achievement.' He added with a wide grin, 'If they ever get fed up with her, they can send her back to me!'

It was evident Ivor appreciated and enjoyed his office. On subsequent visits I was to find him always about his duties, conscious of the need for a well-ordered stable, the comfort of the animals and perhaps an impending public occasion. His kindly nature and devotion to his animals extends to the stable dogs whose

The Harness Room at Ashton Court.

PPB–D

companionship is appreciated and who can also be relied on to help dispose of any vermin.

As Ivor fed Sammy, one of the horses, with a titbit, while two others Matthew and Bloom III looked on inquisitively, I recalled that like people, the horse has also helped to make history. Here were wise and patient souls whose equanimity is not disturbed by din, confusion or vast crowds, or the squeals of delight from the children on the weekly school visits around the city. There were days when the horse was considered too noble to pull the plough. Here were animals handsome and noble enough to share the shafts of the Lord Mayor's coach.

'They like their apple from the Lady Mayoress when we return to the Mansion House after a function,' Ivor said. Then, with a twinkle in his eye, he added, 'And I like my sherry!'

Maxine took down yet another piece of harness for cleaning. Certainly, I thought, no horse could wish for a better master than Ivor, so what was the secret of his success?

'You've got to be either daft or dedicated. Horses come first before family,' he said with a smile. 'Seriously though, without dedication "the horse" would not be here.'

DIDDIE WILLIAMS

Behind the industrious Brislington Trading Estate and not far from the thundering traffic of the Bristol to Bath main road, is a secluded part of Brislington, a reminder of the peaceful country village it once was set in quiet pastureland.

The Chestnuts, a seventeenth-century house, now stands empty in its overgrown grounds, where once, on neatly cut lawns, a game of croquet or bowling would have been enjoyed and from the tennis court would have been heard the 'plop' of ball against racquet. A garden swing, sturdily made, still sits under high mature trees where once the squeak of iron from the suspended seat would have been accompanied by squeals of delight and flapping petticoats. It was here, in 1911, that Edith Williams, always known as Diddie, was born and spent her life until recent circumstances forced her to

Left: *Diddie Williams.*

51

leave the family home for another and more manageable abode not far away in Kenneth Road.

'It was sad leaving,' Diddie said. 'We had such happy times there, but hopefully there is a chance The Chestnuts will be preserved. You see, it became too much for me to keep up and then there was the threat of it being pulled down for the new by-pass. Now Bristol Visual and Environmental Group are interested in it. I must say I am very happy here in Kenneth Road. At one time it used to be a very popular football ground.'

The Chestnuts became the family home in 1879 when Diddie's grandparents moved from Oakenhill Farm just a short distance away. Today, all that remains of the farm is a few derelict outbuildings, but Diddie had heard what life was like at Oakenhill and I was to learn that she has a keen sense of humour as well as knowing a great deal about old Brislington and its people.

'The nearest doctor was on the Coronation Road,' she said. 'When my grandmother was having a baby, someone would have to go a half a mile away to Water Lane to ask Arthur Miller to fetch the doctor. He seemed to be the only one with any transport. Most of grandmother's children were born in the winter and Arthur Miller would complain about it and say, 'I wish Mrs Vowles wouldn't bring her hogs to market in the winter!' Diddie laughed, 'I can only imagine he must have had to wait to take the doctor back after the baby was born. My, how they lived in those days. Near the farm were Oakenhill Cottages. All their water had to be fetched from a well at the farmhouse and carried up a very steep path. No toilet whatever and all waste buried in the garden. One cottage had ten children and wages consisted of sixteen shillings, their cottage and milk. The last daughter died about two years ago and the youngest son is still living. Everything and everyone was spotless you know. The next family who came to live at Oakenhill Farm had twenty children *and* no twins!'

Diddie's grandfather was an architect and her father a Chief Building Inspector involved with work on schools. She was an only child and her parents arranged to have her educated at home with her cousin which was undertaken during the mornings by a Mrs Collins who taught at St Margaret's School in Clifton. I wondered if Diddie had inherited an ability to draw.

'Goodness, no,' she said with a laugh. 'I can't draw at all. If I drew a cat, it would be sure to have two tails and round ears!'

Right: *The Chestnuts today.* Below: *The remains of Oakenhill Farm.*

Principles of living in the past would have been vastly different from today. Community spirit would have been strong, most people co-operating for the benefit of all and Diddie's father was no exception.

'He organised the grass cutting at the Church,' she said. 'He would collect together twenty pairs of shears and sharpen them. Then, on a barrow went the twenty pairs of shears and a cask of cider. He wheeled the lot from The Chestnuts round to St Luke's and everyone would get to work. People had servants then and what the Mistress said was "law" even where their private life was concerned. We had a maid who worked for the family for fifty years. Her name was Kate Merryweather but everyone called her Ginny which was my mother's name, so you can imagine the mix-ups we had. Ginny was amusing from the day she arrived and jumped over the rails of the gate to come up to the house! Sometimes she had to catch Charlie, our pony, to get him in and it would be dark. We had no lights in Brislington and no torches so you can imagine the problem. Poor Ginny would grab around in the dark and then suddenly we would hear her high squeaky voice call out, "I've got him... no it isn't, it's a cow!" When we did have lighting on the roads it was oil. The lamps were cleaned every day and lit every evening by Thomas Beecham who divided his time between lamp-lighting and grave digging. Every lamp had to be lit separately and he carried a ladder which was quite a job on a windy night.'

At Christmas, the kitchen at The Chestnuts would have been a scene of high activity and the puddings were important.

'We had one of those boilers with a fire underneath,' Diddie said. 'The puddings were placed in the boiler and had strings attached to them which hung over the edge so we could pull them out when they were done. They boiled and boiled and then came the inquest when we pulled one out. Was it done? Doesn't look very dark, does it? Oh the palaver, we were all so serious and it was all so funny.' Then Diddie added, 'Do you know you could get ten tons of coal for £10 and that would last us a year!'

When the first world war ended Diddie was seven years old and remembers how the bells rang out and flags went up. 'Everyone was happy,' she said. 'The horse ate one of the flags and I blew a bugle but I don't think I really understood it all.'

Between the wars Diddie grew up and, like many women, stayed at home to help look after the family. At the time, The Chestnuts was still being rented from Mr Alfred Clayfield Ireland, known as The Squire who lived at The Hall.

'Where Crittall's now stands was part of the park of The Hall,' Diddie said. 'There were large iron gates and a lodge at the side. It had a sweeping drive and beautiful lawns. Two huge cedar trees and peacocks and many acres of park and gardens. Teas and entertainment often took place. Mr Ireland was very fond of trees but believed in the old superstition that if the rooks did not build in an elm tree it was not safe. We had about twelve elms in the field in front of the house and every year we would stand and watch in fear in case the rooks did not build in a tree because we knew it would have to come down. We had masses of rooks here then. Mr Ireland was a good landlord though. We used to pay £60 a year, for the

The Chestnuts as it used to be.

An earlier view of Brislington.

house, garden of about an acre and a field. He liked to think he put back the rent by having the paths asphalted and the house colour-washed about every five years. His parents had come to The Chestnuts as a bride and groom and it had been their favourite house. We bought the house when Mr Ireland died for £1500 and a small part of the field for £200. That was in 1923.'

One big amusement to Diddie was the local fire engine which at one time was no more than a cart with a hose attached, manned by local men who would have worked 'down in the city'.

'We could only have a fire when they were home from work,' Diddie laughed. 'Amazingly we never had a house fire and people knew well enough in those days how to put out a chip pan if it caught alight. But there was a time I heard about when some hay caught fire at Scotland Farm. The men pushed and pulled the "cart" up there and when they pumped the water through the hose, it was found to have perished and was full of holes. Water squirted in all directions and the men had a row with the Captain and turned the hose on him. I wonder if they put out the fire! Then they eventually bought a lorry which took half an hour to start sometimes. The funny thing was, they would all dress up in their uniforms and go for a ride on a Monday night. I never knew where though, or why, so it was a good job we didn't have a fire on a Monday night!'

Brislington had its characters and a public house said to be of ill-repute which eventually became Rose Cottage and housed a green parrot with a charmed life.

'Polly was always loose in the garden,' Diddie said. 'One day she flew into the road and a bus went over her. The wheels missed her fortunately, so they stopped, picked her up and put her back in the garden again. It just shows how little traffic there was in those days!

'A real character we had around here was George Humphries who worked on the farms. He was known as Skites and wore an old bowler hat with a green feather at the side. Because he preferred sleeping in the sheds with the pigs, he had been bitten a lot and was a little crippled. One family would let him have a bath and helped to keep his clothes clean once a week but one day he said to my father, "Ooh me feet's bad, Ooh me feet's bad." My father said, "Try washing them," but Skites reply to that was, "That's what's done it!" I expect he washed on other occasions in the pond!'

Haymaking was always met with great excitement. Diddie along with others would spend many hard hours raking up the hay with long wooden rakes. 'First,' she said, 'the grass was cut by two old horses starting at 8 o'clock in the morning and going on until 8 o'clock at night with a short break mid-day. The mowing machine was iron with an iron seat and a little bit of hay on it to make it more comfortable. One man did the mowing and he was about 82 years old *and* very lame. A "tedding" machine shook the hay to dry it in the sun. Then it was made into hay cocks.

'What a joy it was to ride in the hay cart to the farthest end of the field to collect the hay. There were three carts, one an open kind, and I was terrified of falling off it. Another was a little safer with sides and high wooden bars each end and many holes in the floor. Then my favourite had wooden seats along the sides. After the 1914-18 war, a *very* modern piece of equipment was bought! A hay collector with wooden teeth, two wooden handles and two chains. The horse pulled it and collected a lot of hay until it reached the hay rick. Then the man holding the handles threw the whole contraption including the hay near the rick missing the horse and hoping the machine would not "whip" back and hit him!'

After her parents died, Diddie was destined to go on looking after

St Luke's Church where
Diddie was verger.

people. She frequently asked to The Chestnuts for Christmas Day those people from the village she thought might be lonely or even less fortunate. She had learned to understand hardship and the problems of old age and, despite having no real nursing experience, she eventually undertook in the community a caring work which invariably involved people who needed nursing. Her kindly disposition led her not only to the lighting of fires but also to the tying of bandages.

'Grates,' she said with a laugh. 'Always, as long as I remember I seemed to be doing grates. I learned from an early age that grates are either good tempered or otherwise and I knew the value of sugar for making a fire "go". I thought it wasn't noticed until, one day, when I lit the fire for an old lady, a voice behind me said, "So that's what happens to my sugar, is it!"

'One job I had always wanted to do was to be Verger at St Luke's. I was thrilled when I was able to be and I did it for sixteen years. I'll never forget the first wedding I had to attend to. It just *had* to be a Sunday, which was most unusual. I had practised what I had to do for the ceremony and a light at the back of the church had to be pressed for the organ to play when the bride arrived. When the Vicar said "press the light", I pressed it but the bride didn't move. She couldn't because I was standing on her veil! Oh, the brides I have had to contend with, and the mothers, being sick, crying or fainting. Then there was the time there was no water in the font for a christening! It was not always like that though.' Then Diddie smiled. 'The announcements in the paper were certainly differently worded years ago. One local couple who were engaged for 30 years had a wedding announcement which said "after a long and tedious courtship..." and another of a bride said, "she looked pale but lady-like!" '

Although Diddie never married, she has had plenty of children to think about. For forty years she had been secretary to the Church of England Children's Society when Wick House had been a children's home. Despite time and health not permitting her work for others to continue, she busily occupies herself by recording and writing as much as possible of what she can remember of Brislington's past and its people. She also continues to care, as a trace of emotion in her eyes showed, when she applauded the regular and much needed visits to homes in the parish by the present Vicar of St Luke's, Peter Dyson. At the same time, her lively mind was still creating pictures from the past.

'One day my grandfather was walking home and saw a man and a woman fighting. He was a big man and tried to stop the fight but the woman was most indignant at him interfering and said, "Who bist thee, if thee 'ast got a top 'at on?" Well, of course, *all* men wore a top hat in those days!'

TOM BULLOCK

I had often listened to Tom Bullock on local radio telling fascinating anecdotes from Bristol's historic past and giving useful information on antiques. His visits to a place of interest became a visual journey into the past and an appreciation of a less valuable heirloom was met with the same enthusiasm as a rare artifact. It is not surprising he is affectionately known as 'Uncle' Tom Bullock, for his relaxed friendly approach to a subject is always accompanied by a jovial manner and an obvious delight in where or what he is describing.

Tom Bullock - Raconteur.

Only Tom, with his 'winning' way, could have manipulated and set the pattern for the presentation of his programmes over the past four years and, in a large comfortable room at his Stapleton home, Tom's own 'inner sanctum', he told me how he came to take to the 'air waves'.

'It all started in a curious way,' he said. 'I was asked to give a series of ten lectures in Bristol at the Folk House on antiques. One day I was asking a girl in the class what her occupation was and she said she worked at Radio Bristol. A couple of weeks later I was invited to the station to give a talk on antiques and afterwards John Turner, the presenter, said, "Right, next week..." But I said, "Ah, wait, on condition!" When he asked what the conditions were I told him I wanted no strictures, no script. I do it *my* way - so we did.' Then Tom explained.

'You see, whenever Polly Lloyd and I do a programme and, for example, we meet a Curator, I give them a little "pep" talk at first saying it is all very "off the cuff", free and easy and just to be natural. It is important that Polly and I appear as a couple of interested people looking at a museum or whatever, asking questions and generally talking. I like the programme to come over so that people who are unable to go to these places feel they really *are* there and can see things as we do.

'I have done the programme "off the cuff" ever since but...' Here Tom gave a wicked grin, 'I may have said one or two things to raise a few eyebrows! We did a programme in Sun Life once and, referring to a clerk's stool there, I told him it used to have a proper technical name. "What's that?" he said. So I told him it was a "hard arse" stool! It went out over the air but I am sure people take these things in good part.'

Stapleton's Park Road saw the arrival of its future raconteur in 1910 long before the green fields below Pur Down could have foreseen being sliced through by the busy M32 to the city. As a boy Tom attended Rose Green Elementary School and showed a certain promise with essay writing but times were hard in those days and, reluctantly, to the disappointment of Tom and his teachers, he eventually had to leave to look for work.

'It was rather sad,' said Tom, 'but there it was. It is hard to believe now but I was a terribly introverted character you know, terribly shy. Mother would send me out in the morning to look for work and when I got home she would say, "Have you got anything?" and I would say "No, they didn't want anybody," but I hadn't been in! I'd walk round a factory or office building and go home again. Eventually mother got fed up with that, took me by the ear down to Smith Neville's the baker's and I got a job as a "van" boy delivering bread on a horse and cart round the Bishopston area. When I was sixteen I became eligible for insurance, so the firm got rid of me and took on someone else! That was the practice in those days.

'Then I got a job at the old Clare Street cinema as a Commissionaire, probably because I was a big lad and fitted the uniform! I used to stand outside and say "Seats in the 1/9's!" It was rather fun there because it was a very high-class cinema with two restaurants. Upstairs was the Wedgwood Restaurant where the better-class ladies would take tea and buttered teacakes, and downstairs was the Oak Room where the not-so-particular ladies of the city would make rather a fuss of me and pat my cheek! The

Manager, Mr Smart, was very concerned about this and told me he did not think by mother would like to know I could be seen talking to *those* ladies but I did not understand what was wrong because I thought they were rather beautiful you see! I wasn't told either.' Tom laughed, saying, 'Too late now... now I know!'

When the cinema closed down, Tom got a job as a University Scout at Mortimer House, Clifton which he described as 'rather an onerous job of chambermaid, cleaning shoes and emptying pots'! But he soon got fed up with it and applied for a job as a waiter at an hotel in Bournemouth.

'Having waited at table at Mortimer House,' he said, 'I thought I knew all about it and I found out you had to have a dress suit, so I went to a little shop in Boyce's Avenue in Clifton which sold second-hand clothes. I thought I was very lucky when the lady showed me a suit which had belonged to a titled gentleman. It was lined with real canary yellow silk, had frilled shirts and white waistcoats. Worth a fortune it was and I only paid 30 shillings. Off I went but what I didn't know was the suit was not at all the garb of a waiter because they had purpose-made suits and the lady had not told me the titled gentleman had been dead for thirty years! It was hopelessly out of date.

'I eventually found my way round the hotel world and if I had any trouble with the French for soup, I'd simply say, "Thick or thin Sir?" Then I became a head waiter and moved around from hotel to hotel, St Ives, Newquay and Bournemouth. I was hall porter for a time in St Ives and it enabled me to meet a lot of interesting people. One was Sir William Beverage, author of *The Beverage Plan.* He was quite an approachable man and we talked about a great scheme in which everyone would be looked after in a welfare state.'

Tom reflected on the history of Stapleton, telling me about when it was a mining area with mines deeper than Speedwell. People worked hard and lived hard, but there was always a great deal of neighbourliness and everyone used to keep their doors open.

'In the warm weather,' Tom said, 'father used to keep the door open all night and many a time a policeman would call up the stairs to say it was open. Father would call down and say, "It's quite all right, all me gold went down to uncle's years ago." Before the health service there was always someone to help you into the world and someone to close your eyes when you died.

'Back in Victorian times the average amount of milk taken into a

The weir at Stapleton.

household was about a third of a pint a week. It was only to be used for tea, and if you were very poor you bought the skimmed milk from a huge churn which came round on wheels. Milk puddings were a luxury in those days but bread, meat and potatoes were very cheap. If you went to Bristol market on a Saturday night you could get a leg of mutton for a shilling. They couldn't keep it for another day, it would go off so everything had to go. I remember my father telling me of how he and Aunt Mary Anne were sitting in the garden here one Saturday evening when they saw a strange figure coming across the fields. It swayed considerably and was a most peculiar shape. As it got nearer, they saw it was Aunt Mary Anne's husband, Uncle Ted, who having imbibed rather well, had gone into the market for a peace offering which was a six foot long conger eel which he had swung around his neck to cope with the weight of carrying it.'

Tom's father tarred the first road in Bristol and in those days everything was done by hand. 'They had a tar pot,' Tom said. 'It had a canister type engine with a chimney and a fire. The tar was drawn from a tap at the back and was pulled by a very old and patient horse. It moved very slowly as they drew off the tar and

63

literally painted the road. All the women down in Barton Hill used to rush their children out who suffered from whooping cough to smell the fumes. Father also kept a supply of tarred rope at home in case anyone asked for a piece to tie round the neck. He was in charge of a yard at Silverthorne Lane. Butler's tar works were there and the Corporation yard where they heated different sized gravel, tar tops or tar bottoms. The bottoms went as a base to the road and were heated on great iron plates with fires underneath. Then ladles full of tar were poured over it. You see, when I was a small boy, the main roads of Bristol were merely macadamised without any surface covering. In the winter they turned to mud and then froze. In the summer they turned to dust. In the winter three or four men were employed with huge scrapers, about twelve or fourteen feet long, to drag across the road and take the mud off. If it froze on a hill like Whitehall Road, and the traction engines were going to collect bricks from the two brickyards there, the wheels would spin and the women would rush out with buckets of ashes to throw under the wheels and help them up the hill.

'There was a local pub, the "beat'em and whack'em", properly called the Beaufort Arms. They had the finest tug-o-war team in Bristol. Great big husky men who used to train in the back yard with a tripod and pulley, pulling a ton. They beat the police of Somerset, Devon and Gloucestershire. Father told me of Jimmy the Burglar who made his living by collecting rags and things. A most inoffensive and innocent person yet always known by the name because once he illicitly borrowed a shovel or something. There were a lot of very interesting characters around years ago. I remember down in Gloucester Lane in my youth was Charlie Charles. He had a little ice cream shop and he also sold sheet music outside the Empire – fascinating character. Then, too, in Old Market Street was the "flypaper man". He would cry, "Oh those tormenting flies, catch'em alive, catch'em alive".'

Tom's remarkable retention of facts was evident as he recalled many of Bristol's old characters in and around the city. I had always been intrigued by his vast knowledge of antiques and historical matters and had heard him, on another occasion, describe in his inimitable way how "the seat of learning" was invariably to be found in the smallest room in the house. But when did the interest begin?

'It all started when I was working at Stoke Park Hospital as

Group Catering Officer for five hospitals. I took an interest in the hospital itself, the building and estate which goes back to the Conquest, the Giffords, the Berkeleys and later the Beauforts. It became one of the first hospitals for the care of the mentally handicapped. One gift I have is my memory, which can go back to 1913. Now, I can't tell you what day it is today. I can't tell you where I was last Wednesday but if there is anything said or something which has happened, maybe even someone I have met and they have impressed me, it is there for evermore.

'I gave one or two talks on the history of Stoke Park and then people asked me if I talked about anything else. I had always been interested in antiques and had "poked" around in junk shops for years so that had led me to read a great deal about the subject. It is important to have a good memory when reading about dates or who has been involved in furnishing, like Bess of Hardwick or Little Betty Blewer, who learned to make flowers in the potteries for 1s 6d a week. Names like that I remember and even things that have been said, especially poetry. I can remember almost every poem we learned at school. I have given readings on poetry as well as lectures on antiques and I cannot understand people who don't like poetry, they might as well say they don't like songs. I've done talks on Radio Bristol on pills, potions and pirates of the eighteenth century, all fascinating stuff.'

Tom's company is never dull and, from what he told me, neither were his poetry readings for Tom's memory of all he has learned would always include among the more serious facts, an all-important humorous side of life.

'I have always been interested in people,' Tom said. 'I look at someone and I say well, I wonder what *he* does or *she* does. The London tube is magnificent. You sit in there and think to yourself, is he a burglar or a barrister?' Then he added, 'Talking about potions, did you know for rheumatism all you need is water in which a thunderbolt has been boiled?' I looked at him quizzically.

'A bracelet,' he said. 'A special one, made from a coffin handle by the seventh son of a seventh son... but it must be taken from the churchyard at midnight.'

PPB-E

Sportsmen of Bristol

by Jack Russell

ROBERT – 'JACK' – RUSSELL was born at Stroud in 1963. He made his debut for Gloucestershire County Cricket Club v Sri Lanka at the age of 17, when he took 7 catches and made a stumping 'in what must mark as a first-class record wicket-keeper debut' said Grahame Parker in his book Gloucestershire Road. *He has been a professional with the county club since 1980, and many good judges see him as a future England keeper. Jack has written magazine articles on military subjects, but this is his first venture into sports writing. He hopes it will lead to more.*

For hundreds of years sport has flourished in and around this splendid Westcountry city.

Many sporting events have taken place here, and it is the birthplace of numerous sporting personalities. It would need a complete book to cover all of them, but I hope I shall succeed in conveying some of the necessary detail to paint a picture of Bristol sport, past and present.

One of the earliest references to sport can be found in church records of the seventeenth century. At St Mary Redcliffe Church, the churchwarden noted he had seen 'children playing ball in the churchyard'. There were few facilities available for the poor and lower-class citizens of the period, so they made full use of the environment, playing in the streets and in the open land surrounding the city. In particular, the playing of 'fives' and other games in churchyards was common.

Right: *W. G. coming out to bat.*

Many sports, however, began to flourish in the seventeenth century. Archery, dancing, boxing and hunting, plus many others, were very popular. Seventeenth-century maps of the city show the presence of many bowling greens; bowling being a popular sport among the gentry. 'Stobball-play', a game consisting of hitting a large leather ball with a staff, was another popular pastime.

A Bristol journal of 1752 announces 'a cricket match, to be played on 31st August, between XI of Bristol, and XI of London, at Durdham Down, Clifton'. The match was the birth of professional cricket in the area. Cockfighting and bear baiting soon gave way to the new craze of challenge cricket matches, sponsored by local businessmen, and played by professionals. It is interesting to note that sponsorship from local businesses still helps to keep professional and, to a certain extent, club cricket alive. These challenge matches created so much interest that soon local clubs were being formed, one of the earliest being Clifton Cricket Club, in 1819.

It was during this period, in 1808 to be exact, that there was born a gentleman who, in the years to come, was to create great enthusiasm for local cricket, and serve the game admirably during the whole of his life. His name was Henry Mills Grace. So great was his enthusiasm and love for the game, that, while studying to become a doctor, he would get up at four in the morning and make his way to Durdham Downs. There he would meet his friends, and, from 5 a.m. to 8 a.m., would play cricket.

In 1831, he qualified as a doctor, and, with his newly wedded wife, Martha, he moved to the village of Downend. Here they were to have five sons and four daughters. Henry was the first son, born in 1833, and was followed by Alfred (in 1840), Edward Mills (in 1841), William Gilbert (in 1848) and George Frederick (in 1850). They were all born at Downend House, with the possible exception of William Gilbert, W.G., who may have been born at nearby Chestnuts Cottage.

Doctor Henry Mills Grace was to make a considerable contribution to local cricket. He was responsible for the formation of Mangotsfield Cricket Club, in 1844, and two years later he amalgamated the club with Coalpit Heath Cricket Club, to form the West Gloucestershire Cricket Club. The first steps toward County cricket being a part of Bristol had taken place.

By 1850, the Grace family had moved to Chestnuts Cottage, and

The Chestnuts at Downend, possibly the birthplace of W. G. Grace.

it was here that three great cricketing careers began. In the orchards situated behind the house, the Grace boys played cricket, under the watchful eye of their father.

In 1854, on the Black Fields behind the Full Moon public house, at Stokes Croft, the Doctor arranged a match between visiting professionals, an All England XI, and a Gloucestershire XXII. The Doctor captained the home side, with his oldest son playing, and his gardener preparing the field and pitch. Even though the whole twenty-two of the Gloucestershire side fielded, it didn't stop the visitors from winning by an innings and 149 runs. The generous Mr Wintle, the Landlord of the nearby Full Moon public house, sponsored the match with £65 in order to cover the Professionals' expenses. Thus, the first major professional cricket match had been played in Bristol.

It was the first of many to be arranged by the Doctor. The following year an All England XI played here again, and the Gloucestershire XXII lost by 165 runs. On this occasion both Alfred and Edward Mills, E.M., played for the home side. At Clifton Cricket Club in 1856, an All England XI played a 'XXII of Bristol and District'. All England won by 12 runs. The challenge

69

matches created an amazing amount of interest in the area, leading to a spree of clubs being formed in the 1850s. Some of the clubs included Knowle, Frenchay, Bedminster, Bitton, Westbury-on-Trym and Portishead.

In the 1860s, the Doctor turned his attention to matches played by the 'Gentlemen of Gloucestershire'. In 1853 he arranged a match between the Gentlemen of Gloucestershire and the Gentlemen of Devon, played at Durdham Down. This match is believed to be the first ever Gloucestershire County match. It was in the return match, played at Teignbridge, that W.G. played in what is considered his first important match. At the age of fourteen he opened the batting with his elder brother E.M. In August of the same year, the County were to play their first match against local rivals Somerset. The bearded giant's great and amazing cricketing career had begun.

The Grace family on their annual picnic.

England made their first ever tour in 1863, to Australia, but before they travelled, they decided to play a match in Bristol. An All England XI played a XXII of Bristol and District, at Durdham Down, the local side consisting mainly of West Gloucestershire players. Four Graces, E.M., W.G., Alfred, and Henry (junior) played for the victorious home side – an innings and twenty runs the margin.

By now the County Club was beginning to take shape, and it was finally formed in 1870. A year later, the club persuaded the Clifton College Council to let them play cricket at Clifton Close, where the club could charge spectators admission – which they were forbidden to do at Durdham Down. The County were to play there for over 60 years. And it was in the same year that local cricket was to lose one of its greatly loved and respected gentlemen. It was Doctor Henry Grace, who died at the age of 62. A man largely responsible for the introduction of cricket to the area, and a founder member of the Gloucestershire County Cricket Club, he was buried at Downend. Many of the family were to be buried in the same cemetery.

The Graces were a family of doctors, and Henry (junior) and Alfred were drawn away from cricket by their chosen professions. W.G. also studied to be a doctor, but it took him a great deal longer than his brothers, due to his involvement in the game. In 1873, W.G. became the first man in the history of cricket to create any sort of double, by scoring 2139 runs and taking 106 wickets in a season. In the same year E.M. became Secretary to the County Club, a post which he was to hold for 36 years. Early club meetings were held at the White Lion Hotel, today known as The Grand, in Broad Street.

The 1880s were turbulent years for the Grace family. George Frederick died in 1884, and four years later Mrs Martha Grace also died. A match being played at the time between Gloucestershire and Lancashire was deemed to be a draw, 'due to the death of Mrs Grace'. Both were buried at Downend.

By now the County were looking for a suitable ground at which to play their home matches, and make their headquarters. They viewed many plots of land, including sites at Eastville, Redland and Westbury-on-Trym, but they were eventually to settle for a ground at Ashley Down Road, in 1889. W.G. was appointed Director of the Ground Company, and John Spry, the Clifton College gardener

David Allen, one of Gloucestershire's great off-spin bowlers.

was made Head Groundsman. The first ever County match to be played on the County Ground was against Warwickshire. Many sporting facilities were available at the ground, and many clubs and organisations took full advantage. Soon the streets around the ground were developed, and were named after other English cricketing Counties.

A great day occurred at the County Ground in May 1895, a day in which a young Bristol schoolboy was to take part, and never forget. Charles Townsend was the non-striker when W.G. hit the run to give him a century against Somerset, and thus a hundred first-class hundreds. E.M. strolled to the centre of the arena, and poured W.G. a glass of champagne. Play was held up for five minutes while the great man finished his drink.

He played his last match for Gloucestershire in 1899, and the last of his career in 1908, at the grand old age of 60. This great bearded gentleman, who had graced many a cricket field in England and around the world, and whose career record towers above virtually all other cricketers, died in 1915.

The Grace family produced the first of many local born cricketers to become well-known sporting personalities. In recent years, Cotham school has produced three international cricketers.

David Allen was born in Bristol in 1935, and played 39 Tests for England. John Mortimer was another who went on to gain international honours. And there was, of course, the splendid Arthur Milton – a natural ball player, who became the last international double at cricket and football. People who know him have told me that he could have been a professional at a number of sports, including snooker and golf, and he is certainly one of the greatest and best-loved sportsmen ever produced by this city. This quiet man played most of his club cricket at Stapleton Cricket Club, but it was for the 'Willows' that he scored his first century, at the age of thirteen. Five years later he signed as an amateur footballer for Arsenal, and a further five years later, in 1951, he made his debut for them. It was in the same year that he earned his first England Cap, against Austria at Wembley. In 1955 he signed for Bristol City. Three years later he played in his first Test Match, which was against New Zealand at Trent Bridge, where he became only the second Gloucestershire batsman to score a century on their début for England – the first being W.G. in the first ever Test Match in England in 1880. He retired from first-class cricket in

Three Gloucestershire stalwarts, from left to right, Ron Nicholls, John Mortimer and Arthur Milton.

1974, after 26 years, and came close to being one of the first ever paid England selectors. Today he can be seen delivering the local post.

The Ashley Down site remains the headquarters of the County Cricket Club, even though the ground was sold in 1976. The ground still has many facilities, as it did have when it was first bought.

Feelings can rise between North and South County members, some Northern supporters considering the headquarters should be inside the County's borders, and that a ground situated in the North could be developed and made suitable to entertain opposition Counties. I am myself a North of the County lad, but I feel strongly that the ground at Ashley Down should remain the headquarters. Although some of the early matches were played in the North of the County, Gloucestershire County Cricket Club was born in Bristol.

It was a Bristol man who was responsible for its formation, and many of its great sporting personalities were born in the district. A North-of-the-County argument that I often hear on the lips of supporters, as I wander around the home grounds, is that there would be much more support at Cheltenham, Gloucester, and even Moreton-in-the-Marsh. Their point is a fair one, for when the County plays at these grounds the crowd is usually very good. But have they considered whether the crowd attendance would be the same if the County played there all of the time?

Finance is another crucial factor. It would need a large sum of money to buy and develop a ground in the North of the County.

I truly believe that it should stay in Bristol. It has had a long association with the city, which has played a major innings in the club's history and heritage. If the great bearded giant was alive today, I am sure that he would agree.

Rugby Union has also played a major role in the history of Bristol sport. It has been played here for well over a hundred years, with most of the early club sides playing on the large areas of Clifton Downs. In 1888, two of these local clubs, Carlton and Redland Park, joined forces and formed the Bristol Rugby Football Club. Initially, they rented part of the County Ground at Ashley Down, where they played most of their home fixtures. In the 1920s it was decided that a ground should be bought, developed, and made into the headquarters. The plot they finally settled for was at Filton Avenue, Horfield. The Memorial Ground remains the club's headquarters today.

The club has had many international players during its long and fluctuating history. The very first was J. Wallace-Jarmen back in 1900. Len Corbett must be noted as one of the most famous internationals the club has ever had. An England captain, he won 16 caps between 1921 and 1927. He was an entertaining and diverting player, always thrilling the crowd with the unexpected. One such occasion was in the dying seconds of an international against Wales, at Twickenham. Corbett had found himself in a tight and tricky situation. Having hardly any room in which to move, he suddenly passed the ball hard, back through his legs to his wing forward, some yards away, who with plenty of time and space, proceeded to drop a goal and win the match for England. He was also the inventor of elusive swerves and sidesteps, plus the dummy pass.

Another England captain produced by the club was Sam Tucker, a stevedore at the Port of Bristol. An interesting story surrounds one of his internationals. England were playing Wales in Cardiff, but Sam was not playing, he had been dropped from the side a match or two before. At around 12.30 p.m. on the day of the match, he received a phone call instructing him to go to Cardiff and play in the match. Another player had injured himself during a pre-match practice that morning. A train would not get him there on time, so he rushed to nearby Filton Aerodrome, where an open cockpit biplane waited to ferry him to Cardiff. He had never flown before, and was absolutely terrified. There was no airport at Cardiff, so when they arrived, the pilot had to land them in a meadow. Sam made his way to the nearest road, where he flagged down a coal truck, which proceeded to take him to Cardiff Arms Park, arriving five minutes before the start. Sam played a vital role in the winning of the match. He would not have had that problem today, being able to drive over the Severn Bridge and into Wales, reaching Cardiff in less than an hour.

The Bristol club are still producing internationals today, Bob Hesford and Mike Rafter to name but two. One of the most famous and recent Bristol internationals is John Pullin. A local farmer, he played his early rugby for Bristol Saracens, moving to the Memorial Ground in 1961. Five years later, at the age of 24, he made his international debut for England against Wales at Twickenham. He played a total of 42 times for his country, and he is Bristol's most capped rugby international. He still works as a farmer, and can sometimes be heard commentating on club matches for local television.

Surely one of the Bristol Rugby Club's greatest servants is Alan Morely MBE. Born in 1950, the valuer and auctioneer made his debut for the club when he was 18 years old. He has played in 7 internationals for England, and holds the World Record for the most number of tries scored in a career. In 1985 he was awarded the MBE, and is still playing for the club, having now made over 500 appearances.

Right: *The Princess of Wales, Patron of Gloucestershire County Cricket Club hosting a cricket dinner in Bristol in 1985.*

The club is still thriving, with a great deal of success in recent years, including their winning of the John Player Cup in 1982-3, and finishing runners-up the following season to local rivals Bath.

Around the time of the formation of Bristol Rugby Football Club, two more great sporting clubs were born. They were Bristol City and Bristol Rovers Football Clubs.

It was during the football explosion of the late nineteenth century that many clubs were formed in the Bristol region. One of these was the Black Arabs. Founded in 1883, they played their home matches on windswept Purdown. Only a year had passed when the club decided to change its name to Eastville Rovers. In 1892 the Western Football League was formed, and Eastville Rovers became a founder member, along with many other Bristol teams, including Warmley, Bedminster, St George, St Paul's, and Clifton. Two years later they were joined by newly-formed Bristol South End.

Football was immensely popular in Bristol. Such was the enthusiasm of local supporters that, in a match arranged during 1894, between a Bristol and District XI and Sunderland, at Warmley, a crowd of over 9,000 saw the visitors win 9-0. It was during this era that football suffered what is probably its first ever spectator death. It was during a match between Bristol South End and St George that a keen spectator fell to his death from a nearby tree. So distressed was the Bristol South End Club, that they sent £10 to the widow, and the local newspapers organised a fund for the widow and relatives.

It was in 1898 that Eastville Rovers became Bristol Rovers, and a year later they joined the newly formed Southern League. Bristol South End joined the Southern League in the same year, and in doing so, changed their name to Bristol City.

Bristol City finished runners-up in the first year of the competition, and in 1901 merged with Bedminster, and joined the Football League Division Two. Three years later they moved their headquarters from St John's Lane to their present site at Ashton Gate. Today on the St John's Lane site can be found the Dickenson Robinson Group Athletic and Social Club, one of many sports and social clubs that can be found in Bristol.

Just twelve years after its birth, Bristol City were playing in the First Division of the Football League. It is quite interesting to note the players' wages in the early years of the club. They were paid a weekly sum of just £3, and the first manager, Sam Hollis, was given £50 with which to go out and buy new players. In 1906-7 the club finished runner-up in the First Division, and were losing FA Cup semi-finalists two years later.

A famous and much loved player was 'Fatty' Wedlock, reputed to have been one of the most gentlemanly figures ever to have worn an England shirt. He was born near the Ashton Gate Ground and, when he retired from the club in 1921, he moved just across the road to become Licensee of the Star Inn. He died in 1965 at the age of 85.

Bristol City was relegated from Division One in 1910-11, and would have to wait until 1975 before it was to return.

Do not think Bristol Rovers wasn't making a headline or two for itself. In 1920, the Southern League became the Football League Division Three, and Bristol Rovers was a founder member. The club's golden years were certainly the 1950s. They were to produce many giant-killing acts, and have many splendid cup runs. In 1952-3 they reached the Quarter-Finals of the FA Cup. They drew 0-0 away to mighty Newcastle, but stumbled in the replay at Eastville by 1-3. It was in the same year that they became Division Three Champions, and subsequently spent nine successive years in Division Two.

It was during the 1950s that the club operated a 'no buy, no sell' policy, which meant that they were to produce their own local players, and hold onto them. Many fine players resulted, including Harry Bamfoed, Ray Warren, and Bert Hoyle, the jovial goalkeeper, who is believed to have once said to the fans behind him, when things were not going too well, 'Why worry? Once I let in nine against Notts County, and I'm still playing!' Rovers played so well during those glorious 1950s, that they were nearly promoted to Division One.

Today, like most other football clubs, City and Rovers are finding it increasingly difficult financially to keep their heads above water. In 1983 the inevitable happened at Ashton Gate. Bristol City were liquidated, and a new club, Bristol City F.C. 1983 Limited, was formed. Bristol Rovers meanwhile still play at Eastville Stadium, although their offices at present are close to their training ground at Hambrook. There are plans to build a sports complex, including a football stadium, at Stoke Gifford, quite close to the M32 motorway. The local residents, understandably distressed by the

Jack Russell of Gloucestershire County Cricket Club,
who contributed this chapter.

idea, are doing everything they can to put a stop to the project.

Who knows how long it will be before we find British Football Clubs going bankrupt, and disappearing completely? Many clubs are hanging on by their finger tips now! We could see in the future Rovers and City sharing a ground – maybe the stadium at Stoke Gifford, if it is ever built. The amalgamation of the two clubs is not an impossibility. Bristol United perhaps?

Tennis is another keen sport of the region, with numerous tennis clubs, and of course the annual championships at Redland. It was the Bristol High School for Girls that produced Britain's Number One Ladies Tennis Player in 1983, Jo Durie. She was born in Bristol in 1960. Her love for the game was sparked off by summer trips to a relative's house overlooking Lyme Regis Bay. In the grounds of the house was a grass tennis court, and it was here at the age of six that her tennis career began. As the relatives gathered to watch the little girl play, who would know that in future years she would be gracing the great tennis courts of the world.

When she was just eight years old, she joined the King's Tennis Club in Bristol, and it wasn't long before she had won her first-ever tournament, at Burnham-on-Sea. She had a remarkable flair for such a young player, and needed no encouragement. At the age of ten she won the Under Twelve National Championships. In 1976 and 1977 she picked up three National Junior Championships, and by the age of sixteen had won all major Under 18 Championships that there were to win. Soon she was rated as one of the top ten Under 18s in the world. Her career seemed to be blossoming, when she suffered a serious back injury in 1980, which threatened to end her career completely. A spinal operation the same year was successful, and within five months the determined star was back on court. In 1981 she became British Hardcourt Champion, and two years later Britain's number one lady.

In 1983 she reached the semi-finals of the French and American Open Championships, and her career is still going strong. Her future achievements should be watched closely.

Several city-born people have gone on to represent their country in the Olympics. Caroline Holmyard is one. She competed in the Synchronised Swimming Championships at the 1984 Los Angeles Olympics. Her partner in the duet event was Bristol University student Carolyn Wilson.

Caroline made her international debut in 1978, and she went on

PPB–F

to win two World Championships, a duet and team golds at the 1981 European Championships, and was captain of the victorious British team at Rome, in 1983. She retired a year later.

Nick Wilshire is another Bristolian to compete in an Olympics. Educated at St Andrew's Church of England Junior and Portway Comprehensive Schools, Nick played most sports. But it was his brother Luke that persuaded him to take up boxing. When Nick was just eight years old, he joined the National Smelting Company Amateur Boxing Club, at Portbury, and in 1973 he won his first ever contest. He went on to become National Schoolboy and Boys' Club Champion, and one of the youngest ever boxers to win a Senior ABA title. He won a European Gold and World Silver Medal, and represented Great Britain at the 1980 Moscow Olympics.

In 1981 he turned professional, joining Mickey Duff's 'University of Boxers', in London. I am sure that the bare-knuckled Bristol fighters of the early nineteenth century, such as Tom Cribb, the Hanham boxer, and the boxing Member of Parliament, John Gully, would have been proud of him.

All might not have been possible for Nick, had he not survived appendicitis, complicated by gangrene, when he was a small boy. An emergency operation saved his life.

One could not write this chapter without mentioning one of Bristol's most famous sporting personalities of all time. His brilliant amateur and professional career all began on a family holiday to the seaside resort of Bournemouth. While on this holiday, he came across an ice rink, and admiring the colourful posters outside, he begged his mother to take him in and let him have a go. From that day on, this exceptionally talented Bristolian has never looked back.

Robin Cousins was destined to become one of the greatest ice skaters that this country has ever produced. Born in 1957, he was soon attracted to music and dancing. When only four years old he became entranced by the music and movement of ballet. At school he was different from the other boys, preferring music and movement to physical education. When he was nine, Robin wanted to be a ballet dancer, so his parents let him join a ballet club at the Sea Mills Community Centre. He was the only boy in the class, but he was exceptionally good, and his instructor thought that he would have a fine career in dancing when he grew up, if he wished to pursue it. But it was on that Bournemouth holiday that he fell in love with ice skating. Soon he learnt that there was a new ice rink being built in Bristol. For two long years he made anxious visits to Frogmore Street to check on the progress of the builders. When it was finally opened, he skated there regularly, and was soon taking lessons. His first ever coach, Pamela Davis, was to stay with him for eight years, and would take him from being a complete beginner, to European Champion.

In 1964 he entered an Open Novices Championship on Teeside, spending the night before the competition in a caravan. This discomfort was well worth it, as to his surprise, he won. Soon after he received a letter from the National Skating Association, inviting him to attend a coaching scheme at Solihull. The turning point in this young boy's career came in 1970, when he entered a competition to find a future British Olympic Champion. Robin stormed away with the £250 first prize. His next major success came two years later when he won the British Junior Championships. He went from strength to strength, going on to win the Olympic Gold Medal at Lake Placid in 1980.

In the same year he turned professional, and now travels the world performing in ice-skating spectaculars.

Over the past few years, I have grown to love and admire this historical city where I have made my home. It feels as though I am one of many travellers on a sporting journey. A short pause has given me the chance to view the passers by. I can see many sporting personalities, young and old. Their journeys have gone to make up a great sporting story, a story in which, in only a sentence or two, I find myself privileged to be a part.

I sincerely hope the roadway remains clear for new travellers to begin their journeys, so that they can contribute to the continuing Bristol sporting story.

Bristol Inns and Churches
by Jillian Powell

JILLIAN POWELL was educated at Norwich High School and Newnham College, Cambridge, where she was awarded Double First Class Honours in English. After leaving Cambridge, she went on to study the History of Art at the Courtauld Institute, London. She now divides her time between London and the country, working as a freelance writer and teaching English and Art History. In 1985 Jillian contributed two chapters in Westcountry Mysteries, *introduced by Colin Wilson, and recently she wrote* The Quantocks *with photographs by Julia Davey, Bossiney's 120th title.*

Chaucer's Canterbury pilgrims set off from the Tabard Inn at Southwark to make their spring pilgrimage to the shrine of Thomas à Becket in Canterbury Cathedral. In another Medieval poem, *Piers Ploughman*, the figure of Greed is lured into a tavern – where he downs over a gallon of ale – when he should be attending Mass, and Sloth lies snoring in bed while the church bells ring. Whether as poles of virtue and vice, or working in tandem to provide man with physical and spiritual refreshment, inns and churches are rooted together in our Medieval past. And Bristol, once called the 'city of inns and churches', reflects that heritage from almost any viewpoint.

Emerge from the tranquil shade of one of Bristol's splendid churches, and the chances are you will find yourself at the discreet side entrance or back door of one of the city's historic inns. Take a seat outside a pub, like the *Ostrich* in Lower Guinea Street, and you will be beckoned by one or several of Bristol's silvery church

Right: *Author, Jillian Powell.*

84

towers, glimpsed across the rooftops, battlemented or pinnacled, and frequently crowned with the characteristic corner turret over the stairwell. Cheek by jowl, the inns and churches stand together: *St James'* and the *White Hart*, the *Temple* and *Ye Shakespeare*, the *Rummer* and *All Saints*. And beneath the ground, tunnels, rife with stories of smugglers and press gangs, run indiscriminately between inn and church: from the *Hole in the Wall* pub right up to the Church of *St Mary Redcliffe*.

The church and inn are, and always have been, complementary opposites. Both are places where Bristolians congregate and celebrate. City workers find one type of refuge in the cool, hushed interiors of churches like *St Stephen's* and *Christchurch* – pockets of tranquillity in the heart of the city – another in the warm, noisy conviviality of Bristol's many welcoming inns and pubs. In the Middle Ages, the inn provided rest and refreshment (bed and board) for Christian pilgrims, for whom travel was tiring and often hazardous. If they found themselves locked out of St John's Gate at curfew, they could obtain sustenance and shelter at what is now the *White Hart* Inn, standing in the shadow of *St James'* Priory Church, reputed to be the oldest church in Bristol.

A sense of age permeates the cool interior of *St James'*, with its sturdy pillars, round arches and muted stained glass. The five western bays of the Priory's Norman nave have survived, with a fine, mellow façade discreetly decorated with intersecting arches above the windows and interlaced reliefwork running around the small wheel window – the earliest of its kind in England. Across the

86

churchyard, stands the *White Hart*, which was the guest house of the Benedictine Priory from as early as 1480. Its vaulted cellars, which date back to the church's foundation in the twelfth century, back onto the churchyard, and are said to be haunted by the ghost of a man killed by his brother in the old Brewhouse tower, after a quarrel over land. Mysterious sightings and happenings continue at the *White Hart* to this day.

There is a belief that the ghost is kept 'sweet' so long as there are fresh flowers in the house. Nevertheless, he seems to have a prankish sense of humour, which ranges from causing an entire rack

of plates to crack uniformly down the centre, to turning on the flush, taps and hand-drier simultaneously in the Gents' room! Former landlord Geoffrey Rogers, now at the *Angel*, Long Ashton, tells of hearing footsteps upstairs, when the inn was empty, and recalls a story, within living memory, of a priest being called in to exorcise the cellars. The ceremony began, but such a chill, strong wind began to rush through the vaults that the priest was forced to retreat, claiming that the 'presence' was too strong.

Geoffrey Rogers has now left the ghosts behind, but his new pub, the *Angel*, on the corner of Church Road, Long Ashton, has a historical connection with the neighbouring church of *All Saints* which stretches back almost as far as the *White Hart* with *St James'*. In 1495, the *Angel* was given by Sir John Choke, Lord of the Manor of Ashton, to the church as a chantry gift – a church house for the taking of cakes and ales on church festivals. The Choke family arms appear in the stained glass of *All Saints*, a simple country church graced by an intricate oak rood screen, where only the gentle beat of the church clock disturbs the tranquillity. Outside, starlings chatter from the stone battlements, a cockerel crows, and the church bell tolls against the sound of dogs barking and pigs squealing in the farmyard next door. Once, two brew houses, where the church ales were brewed, stood alongside the inn, and a village cross, now in the churchyard, stood outside.

Underneath the *Angel*, are the vaulted cellars where poachers and other malefactors were locked up, awaiting trial by the local Magistrates' court in the Smoke room upstairs. Now, barrels of beer lie in the cool stone cells where they languished – their candle-holds still visible.

The inns' role as coroners' and Magistrates' courts sprang from their connection with the church, for traditionally they were used as church courts, as well as for meetings of the vestry, for the collection of rent and rates from the parishioners.

A church connection which stretches back even further than that of the *Angel* with *All Saints*, is held by the *Rummer*, built on part of a site occupied as early as 1241 by the *Greene Lattis*. That year, the inn was given to the city church of *All Saints* by its owner Alice Hayle, in return for prayers for the repose of her soul. The

Left: *Path leading to St James' Priory.*

churchyard of *All Saints* then extended southward as far as the inn, and in the fifteenth century, when the inn was rebuilt by the church, Thomas Abyndon, a churchwarden, was also innkeeper at his 'local' next door.

The oldest part of the *Rummer* is the cellars, which were under the Medieval hostelry. Landlord Mr Thomas describes the wells used by slaves who were kept down there, and tells of the strange find of an underground kitchen, fitted out with an old cauldron. The cellars run from here under Corn Street, forming part of the maze of tunnels beneath old Bristol.

The *Rummer* itself, rebuilt in the eighteenth century as part of the New Exchange scheme, is imbued with history. Elizabeth I, Charles I and II, William III and Oliver Cromwell are all reputed to have stayed here. During the Civil War, the inn was held first by the Cavaliers, then by the Roundheads, and in the eighteenth century, it became Bristol's first coaching inn, with the first coach arriving after the fifteen hour journey from London, at 11 o'clock on the night of 8 August 1784. From the balcony over the old coach office at the High Street entrance, politicians including Edmund Burke made their speeches, and the inn was frequently the scene of violent brawls between rival political parties.

The Angel (above) *has an historical connection with All Saints Church, Long Ashton* (left).

Now, the *Rummer's* regulars include office workers and porters from the bustling Flower Market which spills along the length of All Saints Lane, vibrant with the scent of carnations and the colourful array of fruit and vegetables.

No less lively is the neighbouring church of *All Saints,* which stands on the corner of High Street and Corn Street, for here, in the imposing setting of a Norman arcade, is a 'classroom in the city' – an exhibition and study centre for Christian and Urban studies. The church was converted in the late 1970s, and now acts as a resources and teaching centre run by Dorothy Jamal and Nick Jones. There is a seminar room and refectory in the old Glebe

91

House or parsonage which is built into the south west corner of the church, and the main nave has been transformed into a lively study area with exhibitions and wall displays, study packs and a library of books and video tapes. Nick Jones says that the children soon get over the initial awe inspired by the spacious church interior with its impressive Norman pillars, round stone arches, and stained glass windows.

Left: *Ye Shakespeare in King Street with Temple Church behind.*

Indeed, in the lively, vociferous atmosphere the children create, it is difficult to imagine the ghost of the Black Monk, a mysterious, cowled figure who is said to have haunted the church for over 400 years. The story dates back to the Reformation, when *All Saints* was one of the treasure houses of the Westcountry, rich with the gifts of pilgrims and the library kept by the monks of the Guild of Kalendaries. At the Dissolution, Henry's officers raided precious crosses, drinking cups, candlesticks and bells, but there was more, they believed – a secret hoard of treasure hidden by one of the monks. They returned, ripping up floors and splitting open pillars – but nothing was found. Legend has it that to this day, the treasure remains hidden, guarded by the Black Monk, who returns periodically to check its safekeeping.

The ghost was first sighted by the vicar of *All Saints,* who saw a cowled member of the Guild of Kalendaries – long after the Guild had been dispersed – gliding down the chancel and disappearing into a stone wall. In 1830, the Black Monk was reported by the vicar and his maid in the parsonage, and over a century later, during a wartime air-raid, a fireworker saw the same, mysterious black figure against one of the church walls. One day, they say, the Black Monk may return to reveal the hiding place of his secret hoard. But when one of Nick Jones' students, working in the office on his own at night, noticed a strange circle of light moving across the church walls, he did not stop to investigate!

All Saints now carries on its new role here in the heart of old Bristol. Yet this is not so much a twentieth-century innovation in the use of redundant churches, as a return to the uses of the Medieval period, when the church was the centre of community life. Today, as then, people of all ages come to learn, to discuss, to share ideas and friendship, as well as to worship. And throughout the city, there are churches playing different roles in the community, some enforced by the devastating bombing of World War II, like the restored shell of the ruined *Temple* Church.

Nowhere are the historical links between Bristol's inns and churches more picturesquely expressed than in the juxtaposition of the crisp, black and white timbered façade of Ye Shakespeare on

King Street, and the mellow, silvery tower of the *Temple* Church rising behind. *Ye Shakespeare,* which bears the date 1636, originally stood on Temple Street. Its windows are filled with Shakespearean ephemera – a doublet and plumed hat, guttered candles and pewter tankards. In the inn's yard, it is said, John Wesley stabled his horse – perhaps while he was preaching in the *Temple* Church next door.

The church is older, founded by the Knights Templar in the twelfth century, and built from the fourteenth century in the soaring, Perpendicular style. Like the famous tower of Pisa, the 114-foot tower leans – 5 feet out of vertical. There is a story that the tower subsided because it was built on wool sacks, a fiction with a grain of truth in it, for the church building was financed by the wealthy wool trade which flourished in this area.

Ironically, it is only the leaning tower which has survived, for during the last war the *Temple* Church was ruined by bombing. The tower remains, deceptively substantial glimpsed from King Street, for behind it is the graceful skeleton of the Perpendicular church, open to the skies. After the war, the church was taken over and restored by the Ministry of Works, now the Department of the Environment, and visitors can obtain a key from the Bristol Boat Centre and wander round this monument of Gothic architecture, picturesquely situated beside the ornamental gardens of Temple Park. Pointed Gothic windows overlap one against another, framing the daylight. Like an architect's drawing in cross section, the *Temple* church unclothes the grace and precision of the Perpendicular style.

Not far away, across Bristol bridge, is the Church of St Nicholas, one of a cluster of churches at the heart of Medieval Bristol, and begun in the thirteenth century on a section of the early town wall. The church was rebuilt in the eighteenth century in the Georgian Gothic style, but one November night in 1940, it too was gutted by bombing, leaving only the tower, crypt and shell of the walls intact. Now, however, *St Nicholas* plays a new, living role in the life of Bristol. In 1973, it was opened by the City Council as a museum of local history and church art.

The visitor passes through a dimly lit room where watercolours and prints of Old Bristol are exhibited alongside glass cases containing silk-embroidered satin chasubles, into the main exhibition and seating area. Here, in a sunny, spacious room

Left: *Landscaped gardens surround St Peter's.*

carpeted in plush, ecclesiastical purple, glass cases glitter with church treasures – silver gilt flagons, candlesticks and trays. The room, dominated by the magnificent triptych painted by Hogarth for *St Mary Redcliffe* in 1755, allows seating for up to 250 people. Here, civic receptions are held, charity events take place and choral and organ recitals are given, as well as the monthly record concerts and private functions.

Upstairs in the gallery, is an illustrated history of Bristol; downstairs, in the cool of the rib-vaulted crypt, is a brass rubbing centre. Here, the annual carol service is held, and every November, the girls of the Red Maids' School come in pilgrimage, bearing candles to the tomb of their founder, John Whitson. Amidst all this activity, the church remains consecrated for Christian services, and its bells still ring the curfew at nine p.m. as they have done since Medieval times.

St Nicholas' tower can be seen from across the Green, where two more churches devastated by wartime bombing stand, performing their own role in the Bristol landscape. *St Peter's,* traditionally the mother church of Bristol, may occupy the site first used in the town for a religious building. Its surviving structure is early Perpendicular of the fifteenth century. Across the Floating Harbour is the Courage Brewery. On a crisp, October morning, clouds of vapour rise from every rooftop chimney, every pipe and window vent. Young and old sit, enjoying the sheltered spaces between the church buttresses, reading, knitting, or just enjoying the view and the scent of lavender from the landscaped gardens which surround *St Peter's*.

From here, a cluster of church towers is visible, and a stone's throw away, across the Green, is the late Medieval Church of *St Mary's*. Only the Perpendicular west tower survives, with its characteristic Bristol corner pinnacle above the stairway turret. Hemmed in by office blocks, the tower stands isolated like the past surrounded by the present. It offers city workers and visitors an oasis of peace and quiet, with shady seats placed against a low wall whose stones reveal the jigsaw of a broken gravestone.

No less than *All Saints* or *St Nicholas,* these churches play their role in the life of Bristolians, and remain as poignant reminders of Bristol's losses in the war. Elsewhere in the city, those losses have become the starting point for new ideas and new architecture, as in the church of *All Saints* in Pembroke Road, Clifton, where the past, in the form of the nineteenth-century church by George Street, which was severely damaged in the war, has been imaginatively blended with twentieth-century design and materials. The exterior displays a fusion of old and new, with Street's grey and rust stone tower surmounted by a streamlined, laminated timber spire clad in aluminium. The tower now acts as a porch, and the visitor enters not into shadowy darkness, but into a light, airy glazed cloister or atrium. One door leads into the secluded church garden, another into the main nave which is full of light and colour as the sun streams through brilliant, fibreglass windows onto the clear ash woodwork and natural stone. At the west end, the stone font stands awash with blue light from the windows symbolising the Tree of Life and the River of Life, by John Piper. New life, it seems, has been breathed into the older church, burned out on the night of 2 December 1940.

But for some, like the eighteenth-century Church of *St Nicholas*

Right: *Taking the sun at St Peter's.*

Above and Right: *Viewed from St Peter's - the Courage Brewery and a cluster of church towers across Bristol Bridge.*

and Leonard by Bristol Bridge, the damage was irreparable. Only the treasures stored in the crypt, and including a pair of priceless Queen Anne wrought-iron gates by William Edney, survived the bombing. Now, however, *St Nicholas and Leonard* lives on as part of the new city parish with *St Stephen's* and *All Saints*. And in the north aisle of the church of *St Stephen's*, in St Stephen's Street, is a quiet chapel, paved in York stone, and presided over by the figures of St Nicholas and St Leonard, carved in high relief from a wall of Bath stone. The chapel, which was opened in 1960, is entered by Edney's magnificent wrought-iron gates, and here, too, is the sword rest by him, another treasure rescued from the ruined church.

St Stephen's, with its splendid, pinnacled tower admired by Ruskin, is the new parish church of the city of Bristol. The tower stands 130 feet high, with the richly traceried pinnacles and openwork crown which are characteristic of richer towers in the Bristol Channel area. It was built in the fifteenth century, financed largely by the wealthy merchant family of the Shipwards, and today

A stained glass window in St Mary Redcliffe.

St Stephen's retains its seafaring connections, for the Rector has pastoral responsibility not only for the city, but for all the waters of the Port of Bristol, up to Walton Bay and the islands of Steep Holm and Flat Holm. Ships used to pass right by the church when the Floating Harbour infiltrated the city centre through to the site of Colston Avenue. Now, as well as the banks, businesses and civic societies who hold services here, the seamen hold a service every Trafalgar Sunday, in this church which has long been associated with the Merchant Venturers.

Their arms surmount the elaborate monument to Martin Pring, the seventeenth-century navigator and explorer who discovered Cape Cod Bay in Massachusetts. 'He made humility a ship, Religion his only Compass... Faith was his sails, his anchor hope', reads a tablet supported by two colourful figures of a mermaid and merman, who would look as much at home on a ship's prow, or an inn sign, as on a church memorial.

Bristol's seafaring history is all around, here in *St Stephen's* as in inns like the *Llandoger Trow* or the *Hole in the Wall*, which have been the haunt of seafaring men for centuries. *The Hole in the Wall* in the Grove is sometimes claimed to be the original for the Spy Glass inn, in Robert Louis Stevenson's *Treasure Island.* It is now a Berni inn – which Aldo Berni remembers as the inn he acquired on the day he coincidentally achieved a 'Hole in One' on the golf course! It still retains the 'Long John Bar', but its most interesting feature is undoubtedly the 4-foot square spy house which juts out from the front of the building, overlooking the waterfront. In the eighteenth century, the inn was subject to ruthless raids by the Press Gang. From here, a regular watch was kept on the quayside, to warn sailors drinking in the bar, who could escape through a passage at the back into Queen Square, or seek refuge in the maze of underground tunnels which run from here to the *Llandoger* and right up to the church of *St Mary Redcliffe. St Mary Redcliffe,* too, shares in this seafaring history, for here generations of wealthy merchants of the Port of Bristol began and ended their voyages at the shrine of Our Lady of Redcliffe. Here, too, is the tomb of William Canynges, Bristol merchant and priest of *St Mary's,* who financed the restoration of the church in the fifteenth century.

Above all, *St Mary's* is a parish church, described by Queen Elizabeth I as 'the fairest, goodliest and most famous parish church in all England'. It serves parochial needs today, as it has done since the Middle Ages. On a bright October morning, parishioners leaving the Sunday service spill down the limetree avenues leading from the south entrance. Sidesmen sit chatting, the choir disperses. Here, the Guides and Scouts meet weekly, organ recitals are held, the Guild of Bellringers meet for practice, the Mother's Union for coffee and chat. From the 'Academy' orchestra and chamber choir to Redcliffe Care for the Old, the church continues its active role in the community, retaining close links with the Bristol General Hospital and the Church School of St Mary Redcliffe and Temple in Somerset Square. Standing high on the hill, with its soaring, Perpendicular lines and crisp, floriate decoration, this fine parish church bears witness to Bristol's merchant prosperity in the Middle Ages.

It was the prosperity of Bristol's merchants which, in the seventeenth century, gave rise to the line of fine, timber-framed houses built along King Street, close to the Welsh Back quayside. No. 5 became the *Llandoger Trow,* an inn which, as E.V. Thompson describes in his Introduction, is still redolent of sea shanties and

seafaring folk. Within living memory, boats have arrived here from Dublin, carrying their cargo of Irish Guinness, and the barrels have been rolled along the flagstones outside the *Llandoger*, right up to the *Naval Volunteer*, another seafarer's haunt, once reputed to draw drinkers from miles around. Some regulars have been coming to the *Llandoger* for forty years or more. One, a Dutchman, can remember the very day, and hour, he first walked in, for on 9 October 1942, he had gone with his fiancée to arrange a date for their wedding with the Registrar, and had returned to the *Llandoger* a married man – such were the contingencies of wartime!

The *Llandoger* takes its name from the flat-bottomed sailing barges used by merchants like Captain Hawkins, who traded from the nearby Welsh Back, perhaps with the village of Llandogo on the Wye. Quayside inns like the *Llandoger* were the haunt of the Trow owners, and were used as meeting places for the recruitment of sailors and ship hands, or emigrants to the New World. Many, like the *Three Mariners,* and the *General Blakeney* have gone. *The Llandoger* remains, imbued with stories of the slave trade, of

Below: *Sunday lunchtime outside the Llandoger Trow and the Old Duke.* Left: *The Cathedral Church provides a fitting setting for Legal Sunday.*

smuggling and piracy, of secret passages and the Press Gang. Its very gables seem to lean towards the waterfront. Inside, the famous black ceiling is said to have been painted over by the landlady, a prudish widow who was tired of the sailors ogling the decorative nudes which once adorned it! Like the *Hole in the Wall*, the *Llandoger* claims to have been the original Spy Glass inn in *Treasure Island*, and here, it is said, Daniel Defoe, who described Bristol as the 'richest and greatest port outside London', met Alexander Selkirk, who inspired him to write *Robinson Crusoe*.

In Bristol Cathedral is a pair of silver candlesticks, dated 1712, which were given by one of the promoters of the privateering voyage under Woodes Rogers, who rescued Alexander Selkirk from his castaway island. Like *St Mary Redcliffe*, the Cathedral church is rooted in Bristol's prosperous Medieval past, founded in the twelfth century as part of St Augustine's Abbey, one of Bristol's four Medieval friaries. Standing on College Green, opposite the sweeping, 1930s façade of the Council House, the Cathedral provides a fit setting for occasions like Legal Sunday, with the pageantry of the Lord Mayor's coach and the official robes of civic and legal dignitaries, with their plumed hats or black gaiters and white cravats.

Such pageantry is a conscious preservation of the past – like the gesture made by Courage Breweries in sprinkling the floor of Clifton's *Coronation Tap* with sawdust. But if the sawdust-scuffed floor of this famous old cider house is a deceptively 'historical' innovation, there are regulars like Len and John in the pub, who remember the 'spit and sawdust' pubs with their 'spittoons' or copper bowls for tobacco on the floor of the public bar.

Over a pint of cider, Len and John remember the landlord who refused to serve ladies with pints, and did not allow men and women to hold hands in his bar. And if any customer dared to ask for a pint of 'scrumpy', he would be told in no uncertain terms that the landlord served cider, not 'scrumpy'. Len and John have been coming to the *Coronation Tap* in Sion Place for many years, long enough to remember characters like the Irishman Eamonn who, after a pint or two of cider, would treat regulars to a rendering of *Widecombe Fair*. And if they remain unimpressed by the recent

Right: *Legal Sunday at the Council House.*

Left: *The Ostrich, an eighteenth-century coaching inn.*
Above: *The river view from The Ostrich.*

appearance of sawdust on the floor, they are nevertheless fondly possessive of their local, and sensitive to changes. Over in Westbury on Trym, when Falstaff Inns proposed renovations to the *White Lion* which included partitioning off part of the bar as a restaurant area, 890 regulars, led by Clive Hirst, signed a petition opposing the changes, took the case to court, and won back a few valued feet of their bar space. Not far away, in the parish church, whose origins go back to the early ninth century, the sound of hammering and singing indicates that here, too, renovation work is in progress, for the church has just reached its target of a £100,000 roof appeal.

Churches and inns grow, and change – or die – with the communities they serve. Gone are the days when travellers slept four to a room in bedrooms with names like 'The Rose Chamber' and 'The Pomegranate' at the *Swan Inn* which stood for 500 years at the junction of Mary Le Port Street and Dolphin Street. Bristol lost *The Swan* in 1936, but other inns survive, serving new communities. In Lower Guinea Street, the eighteenth-century

coaching inn of the *Ostrich*, with its oyster-washed façade, bright hanging baskets and landscaped waterfront, has become part of Bristol's dockside revival. Here, city workers gather to enjoy a drink and a river view bristling with ships' masts which recall the sea captains who once had their homes in nearby Guinea Street. And by the *Llandoger* on the Welsh Back quayside, where once recruits assembled for the privateers, or bounty was shared amongst the homecomers, families and friends sit on a Sunday lunchtime, listening to live jazz from the *Old Duke*, while bemused pigeons look down from the rooftops and window ledges.

As times change, so do the inns and churches. Their history is the history of Bristol: the rise of the merchant classes in the Middle Ages, privateering and the slave trade, eighteenth-century and Victorian prosperity. In Henbury churchyard is the grave of Scipio Africanus, the beloved negro slave of the seventh Earl of Suffolk, while the *Seven Stars* Inn, by *St Thomas'* Church, is the place where the Reverend Thomas Clarkson gathered evidence to support William Wilberforce's act for the abolition of slavery. The eighteenth-century wealth which is reflected in the graceful white and gilt interior of *Christchurch with St Ewen*, also gave rise to the many coaching inns which then flourished, like the *Angel* at Long Ashton on the busy turnpike road from Bristol to North Somerset, the *Greyhound* in Broadmead, or the *Albion*, tucked away off Boyce's Avenue, Clifton, and recalling the prosperity of the Hotwell Spa and Boyce's speculative building schemes.

The golden age of coaching inns has long since gone, but pubs like the *Albion* can still tell a story or two. Recently, the *Albion* came into the news as the intimate setting where Bristol M15 Double Agent Peter Edge met his contacts. Landlord Gerald Gilling has had his name in the papers, too. When his wife Pam, driven to desperation by his loud snoring, locked him out in the yard one night, twenty-two stone Gerald dozed off on a table – and made so much noise that the police were called to investigate! Unabashed, Gerald has framed the story for the walls of the *Albion*, a pub whose exterior, with its narrow cobbled courtyard flanked by stables, has changed little since Boyce's time.

Left: *The Albion and landlord Gerald Gilling.*

Alongside the old, the new grows up, symbolised on an awe-inspiring scale by Clifton's new Catholic Cathedral of SS Peter and Paul, in Clifton Park, built in the early 1970s. Standing among copper beeches and sycamore trees, with its blind walls clad in pink Aberdeen granite, and its 165 foot concrete flèche, the Cathedral is a bold twentieth-century statement amidst Bristol's historic architecture. Inside, daylight floods in through hidden rooflights onto a light and spacious interior, designed around the geometry of helix, fan and hexagon.

Design has changed, materials have changed, even the approach to liturgical worship has changed. But as new buildings grow up, and others are restored, or sadly lost, the inn and the church remain twin foci of the community, complementary opposites in the life of Bristolians, as they have been since Chaucer wrote his *Canterbury Tales,* in the Middle Ages.

Also Available

UNKNOWN BRISTOL
by Rosemary Clinch
Introduced by David Foot, this is Bossiney's first Bristol title. 'Rosemary Clinch relishes looking round the corners and under the pavement stones ...'
'... with its splendid introduction by David Foot, peeps into parts of Bristol that other books do not, and I can hardly do better than steal from David's introduction a quote from that great journalist, the late James Cameron, who declared to the editors of the many papers for which he worked, "If you want the facts, you can get 'em from Reuters. I'll look beyond the facts for you." In her own way this is exactly what Rosemary Clinch has done for Bristol ...'
Heidi Best, Somerset & Avon Life

UNKNOWN SOMERSET
by Rosemary Clinch and Michael Williams.
A journey across Somerset, visiting off-the-beaten-track places of interest. Many specially commissioned photographs by Julia Davey add to the spirit of adventure.
'Magical Somerset ... from ley lines to fork-bending; a journey into the unknown ... a guide which makes an Ordnance Survey map "an investment in adventure".'
Western Daily Press

CURIOSITIES OF SOMERSET
by Lornie Leete-Hodge
A look at some of the unusual and sometimes strange aspects of Somerset.
'Words and pictures combine to capture that unique quality that is Somerset.'
Western Gazette

GHOSTS OF SOMERSET
by Peter Underwood
The President of the Ghost Club completes a hat-trick of hauntings for Bossiney.
'... many spirits that have sent shivers down the spines over the years ...'
Somerset County Gazette

THE QUANTOCKS
by Jillian Powell with photographs by Julia Davey
'Seen from Taunton or The Mendips, the Quantocks look timeless ...'
Sensitive combination of words and pictures produce a delightful portrait of the area.

SOMERSET IN THE OLD DAYS
by David Young. 145 old photographs.
David Young of TSW takes a journey in words and old pictures across Somerset.
'Scores of old photographs of good quality and high human interest... Excellent value... It is narrated by David Young, Television South West's architectural pundit, and his captions are usually eye-catching and informative.'
Drew Brodbeck,
Gloucestershire and Avon Life

STRANGE SOMERSET STORIES

Introduced by David Foot with chapters by Ray Waddon, Jack Hurley, Lornie Leete-Hodge, Hilary Wreford, David Foot, Rosemary Clinch and Michael Williams.

'Publisher Michael Williams has tried to capture an essence of the Westcountry bizarre ...'

Peter John,
Bath and West Evening Chronicle

LEGENDS OF SOMERSET

by Sally Jones. 65 photographs and drawings.
Sally Jones travels across rich legendary landscapes. Words, drawings and photographs all combine to evoke a spirit of adventure.

'On the misty lands of the Somerset plain – as Sally Jones makes clear – history, legend and fantasy are inextricably mixed.'

Dan Lees, The Western Daily Press

PEOPLE & PLACES IN DEVON

by Monica Wyatt
Dame Agatha Christie, Sir Francis Chichester, Dr David Owen, Prince Charles and others. Monica Wyatt writes about eleven famous people who have contributed richly to the Devon scene.

'A very interesting title from this rapidly expanding publishing house. Indeed, for a "cottage" industry it's going from strength to strength, its territory now covering an area from Bristol to Land's End.'

Irene Roberts, The South Hams
Newspapers

PEOPLE AND PLACES IN CORNWALL

by Michael Williams
Featuring Sir John Betjeman, Marika Hanbury Tenison, Barbara Hepworth and seven other characters, all of whom contributed richly to the Cornish scene.

'... outlines ten notable characters ... whose lives and work have been influenced by "Cornwall's genius to fire creativity"... a fascinating study.'

The Cornish Guardian

EXMOOR IN THE OLD DAYS

by Rosemary Anne Lauder. 147 photographs.
The author perceptively shows that Exmoor is not only the most beautiful of our Westcountry moors but is also rich in history and character: a world of its own in fact.

'... a wealth of old postcards, old pictures and words aglow with warmth ...'

Western Evening Herald

We shall be pleased to send you our catalogue giving full details of our growing list of titles for Devon, Cornwall and Somerset and forthcoming publications.

If you have difficulty in obtaining our titles, write direct to Bossiney Books, Land's End, St Teath, Bodmin, Cornwall.